The House
I Left
Behind

By the same author

Christ Above All:
Conversational Evangelism with People of Other Faiths

Islam and the Son of God

For more information on Daniel Shayesteh's books

www.exodusfromdarkness.org

7spirits@gmail.com

The House
I Left
Behind

A journey from Islam to Christ

by **DANIEL SHAYESTEH**

Talesh Books

Scripture taken from the New King James Version.
Copyright © 1982 by Thomas Nelson, Inc. Used by
permission. All rights reserved.

Daniel Shayesteh, 1954–
The house I left behind: a journey from Islam to
Christ
Published by Talesh Books, Sydney, Australia.
ISBN: 978-0-9756017-4-7

A previous version of this book was
published as *Islam the House I left Behind*.

Talesh Books are distributed in the USA
and internationally by Ingram Book Group:
orders@ingrambook.com

DEDICATION

I dedicate this book to all those who had no choice
but to flee their homes.

ACKNOWLEDGMENTS

Endless appreciation goes out to those who prayed
for the completion of this book, and the editors who
helped me express my personal and cultural feelings.

— Daniel Shayesteh

Contents

Author's Preface

It was difficult for me to leave my house and hometown, especially when I could not tell my family that I may never see them again. I could not reveal my secrets. My family is big, and if I told them, the news would spread and possibly hinder my departure.

It has been over two decades since I have seen my family. It has been especially hard between my mother and me. We have cried many of days and nights throughout the years, wishing to see each other. Many Iranians gather together in stranger lands and recite their heart melting poems about their mothers. "Iran is watered by the tears of my mother; I have a right to call it my motherland," is the common complaint of many who were forced to leave their families behind.

The Islamic Republic of Iran has built many doors between Iranian parents and their children. The doors get closed to all if just one member of a family opposes government. For this reason, millions of doors are closed now between the children of Iran and their parents. The Islamic government has left a lot of parents mourning for their lost and fugitive children.

It is not even easy for many of us to communicate with our families through telephone, e-mail or letters. Everything is checked and limited by the government. A mother can be tortured for having communication with her son or daughter who is an opposition to government. The Muslim rulers take delight in hurting those who do not align themselves with their Islamic theocracy.

Some years ago, an Asian man met me in a seminar, which I was running in a European country, and said that he had planned to visit Iran. He also said that on the way to visit his friends, he would drive through my hometown Talesh. He was trying to do me a favor—since I had not seen my family for many years—and take my message to my family. I gave him an address and also a small photo of mine so that he could present that photo and prove that he was a friend but not an agent of Iranian Government. The fear from the government is huge in Iran and people do not trust others easily. However, he visited my nominated familial person. After leaving Iran, he wrote to me and said that my sibling was not able to speak to him openly inside the house but took him out so that they could talk freely. When they were walking and talking in a park, my sibling stared at my photo, wept and said, "Tell my brother that Iran, the land of our forefathers, is a prison for us now. Even in our houses we do not dare to express our concerns, fearing that the words may get out via our little children."

This is what our motherland is experiencing now; fear and torture. This pierces our hearts. We are not only suffering of separation, but from the pains of our families too.

For this reason, we have no choice but to pray and also speak out. My family's life is changed now and our mind-set is different. We believe in Christ now. We have learned to not respond to the cruelty of Islamists in Iran as they responded to us and millions of other Iranians. We pray for Islamists every day that they might see the glory of loving Jesus and start respecting people regardless of race, nationality or belief. Iran needs to put religious and human hostility and revenge aside and make the unconditional love of Christ the ruling power in its life in order to pave the ground for unity.

We have suffered while traveling the valleys and mountains of our lives. Our minds and hearts are now established on a heavenly ground, and our souls soar in high places by the power of Jesus Christ. We need to focus on Him more in order to love people who are caught in the claws of hostile beliefs.

This will help us to climb beyond the veils and weaknesses of our flesh and grasp the full beauty of the One who saved and taught us that only love creates peace among people.

I am convinced that I should allow the unconditional love of Christ to shape my life with kindness, respect and forgiveness if I desire to live in peace with others. Unconditional love removes every barrier and unites sincerely. This is the reason for me to put my life story in words and show others how Jesus brought me out of hostility into His love so that I could respect and bless others. I did not know that I needed to use my freedom of choice, open my eyes, know my Creator, align myself with His absolute truth and present myself as a blessing to others. I did not know that I was walking in a path so far from God. I was ignorant and therefore was easily misled and kept away from the real peace which God has created me for. But my Creator had not forgotten me. He was planning to unchain me so that I could rest in Him and have fellowship with others through Him. This what my book is trying to convey.

My prayer is that this book, *The House I Left Behind*, will work as an educational tool, encouraging many to give up passivity or hostility and yearn for the peace of Christ. I also pray that it will become an encouraging testimony to many so that they will exalt the Name of Jesus Christ, who is the Author of my life.

Daniel Shayesteh

Leave in Order to Live

*The Lord had said to Abram, "Leave **your** country, **your** people and **your father's household** and go to the land I will show you." (Genesis 12:1)*

I should have died, many times over. But God had a plan for me to live and to proclaim that He is the Sovereign One: The One who commands all things. If He plans for you to live, He Himself opens the door for life, even to escape the hands of death.

The Ayatollah Khomeini, the grand leader of Iran, sentenced me to death because I dared to oppose him, but God cancelled his plan and rescued me from Khomeini's dark cell of death. There were other great deliverances by His Mighty hand: The Religious Guards of Iran tried to murder me by running me down. I was struck by a car and fell down a ravine. They left me for dead but, again, I remained alive. I was meant to fulfill purposes that, at that time I had no idea were planned for me from eternity past. Thankfully, I was discovered and was looked after until I recovered. I knew then that I had to leave Iran and escape to Turkey. Still, in Turkey I found no safety from the enemy: Here, too, God saved me twice from certain death: once from the agents of the Islamic Republic of Iran and the second time from the hands of twelve Turkish radical Muslims who sought to end my life for naming the name of Jesus Christ.

I sought knowledge in Turkey, during these early days of my life. I was able to come face-to-face with the values and beliefs of other cultures. The opportunities I was given opened my eyes to evaluate my own religious, social and moral values and to contrast them with others' ways of thinking. In this manner I was able to leave the spiritual house that had chained me to a dogmatic belief system which rejected the rights of all nations, especially those that were not intrinsically Islamic.

It was not until I became a follower of Christ that I was able to recognize the intolerance and inhumanity of my own religion. This is really not surprising, since Islam has always been determined to isolate itself from outside influence. If it had not been for Christ, I would have remained unfamiliar with other cultures and beliefs. However I realized that I could never be completely free, spiritually speaking, unless I took the time to understand the Truth in the context of the world. I was determined to study the values esteemed by other people groups so that I could fully understand the superiority of the knowledge God had revealed to me.

I was awakened to a new fascination with my own country. I was increasingly interested in the history and culture that was my birthright, but that I had neglected. This journey opened my eyes to realize that God, in many ways, has prepared witnesses for His own glory among all nations. This was something I found to be true not only in Iranian (Persian) culture but throughout every culture that I investigated. God's aim is to magnify Himself, to open the eyes of people to understand His loving kindness toward them and His desire for reconciliation and unity with sinners:

> *For His invisible attributes, namely, His eternal power and divine nature, have been clearly perceived, ever since the creation of the world, in the things that have been made.* (Romans 1:20)

I was blessed to discover that God had prepared divine witness in Iranian culture that has been kept alive through tradition for thousands of years. He did this by His sovereign grace in order to raise people for Himself from among the nation of Iran.

Because God revealed to me through my studies that He displayed His glory for all men to see, I was spiritually prepared to respect the rights of all nations no matter how backward or advanced I had once perceived them to be. I knew that God had determined that His glory, through the witness of creation, was for all men to see in order to relate Himself to humanity.

My mind has been opened to understand that as humanity is able to see the work of God in all things that revelation is able to remove the mountains of ignorance and hatred that separates nations. Praise God for such a revelation that changed and rescued me from the house of hatred. My eyes are open now. I cannot believe, because of God's Spirit that dwells in me, that I am a creature superior to others, whether they are Jews or any other people group, as Islam had taught me. The Quran was once the law by which I lived, laboring in utter darkness, but now I have found the one true God in whose eyes all peoples are the same.

BORN
TO RUN
ALL THE
WAY

1

His Witness in my Hometown

I was born in the countryside village of Talesh or Tavalesh, located on the Western edge of the Caspian Sea in northern Iran, a country which was once the kingdom of Persia. Geographically, Talesh is the largest territory in the state of Gilan, with high snowy mountain peaks, dark rainy jungles, and rice plateaus. It is a beautiful place for those who love nature. The language of the people is Taleshi, which belongs to the Indo-European family of languages. Historians believe, Taleshis could be the first Aryans, or pre-Aryan nation, to inhabit the northern parts of Ancient Persia, surrounding the Caspian Sea.

The Taleshis are an agrarian culture whose main source of revenue is farming rice, sheep, and cattle. Rice farmers are found on the plains surrounding the Caspian Sea, while the sheep farmers tend their flocks in the foothills of the mountains to the west.

Talesh preserved its own unique culture despite the invasion of Muslim Arabs in the seventh century AD. There was a great struggle between the Iranian people and invading nomadic Arabic culture. Iranians, including Taleshis, treasure their national heritage and values, which stood in stark contrast to Islamic culture and its religious fundamentalism.

From what we know of early Taleshis' religious practices, they did not have any interest in Islam, and defended their culture from change for centuries. It was not until the 12th century AD that the Safavid Dynasty (the kingdom of Iranian Turks or Azeris) forced Islam on Iran (Persia). Iran now may appear to have always been Muslim. However, according to Iranian history this is not true.

Because of pressure from the invading forces, and the rise of Islam, Taleshis never used their language in Islamic religious ceremonies. Religious ceremonies, sermons and mourning were all performed in the Azeri language, for Shiites only. The Taleshis' native culture and dress code indicate they never desired to align themselves with Islam.

Taleshis adhered to powerful cultural values for thousands of years despite many invasions. Only Islam created a separation, as some Taleshis are Shiites and some are Sunnis. This segregation was obvious only among committed Muslims. Many Shiite and Sunni Taleshis prized their culture and language far more than the values of Islam, and they lived amicably side by side.

Song of the Bulls

Music and song are vital to the culture of my homeland. Taleshis love both music and singing. Music has the ability to move and touch the hearts of all Taleshis. Their love affair with song does not stop at man-made music. It includes the music of nature, birds and all creatures. This is a blessed legacy inherited from their forefathers, and from God.

Music is the strongest language among the Taleshis. It is this love and open-heartedness that enables them to hear even the song of a bull or a cuckoo. Yes, Taleshi bulls sing.[1] They

---

1   The word used to describe the song that a bull sings is "Vang". Vang means to sing in order to get attention. Not only does the singer try to get attention, but there is also a cultural expectation that the hearer heeds the call.

sing with a beautiful melodious lowing. Some can sing for a full minute. Such a song will bring tears to the eyes of native Taleshis. Perhaps this is reminiscent of a time before man's disastrous fall into sin. Perhaps Adam was able to communicate with animals in a way that is scarcely imaginable now?

When a Taleshi bull sings or a cuckoo raises its voice, countrymen sing in response, "*jon brom jon,*" or "*jon nanam jon*" or "*jon cuckoo jon,*" which means, "My brother or my mother (for a singing cow) or dear cuckoo, I am ready to give my life for you so that you might be able to live long and sing longer." This does not mean that a person is literally ready to die for a bull or a bird, but it expresses the depth of peaceful unity that such songs inspire. It shows how the soul can be moved by God's creation. Humanity's soul should indeed be moved by God's creation.

Some animals seem to understand that there are people who care for their songs. They seem to know that songs can touch the hearts of humanity. They sing to provoke people to sing, and they sing for their masters, to receive the best treatment. In Taleshi country, if you hear the song of the bull you may soon hear the sound of a person's voice responding. This is similar to social gatherings, where songs sung and the recitation of poems is often an inspiration for others to sing and recite in response.

Masters talk to animals and animals to their masters. They understand each other. As people learn from animals, animals also are sometimes able to learn from people in order to establish a channel of communication to have their needs met. For example, if the master is late in bringing a cow's calf to her, she sings in order to draw his attention. Bulls and cows returning from a day of grazing sing to announce their return or their need for water or more food. If the master is late, many cows will sing in turn or sometimes together, expressing the urgency of their immediate needs. Owners may express empathy with soothing words, saying, "What, what, am I late? Are you hungry or thirsty?" The cow that loses her calf cannot be comforted, crying a song of distress for days in hopes that her owner will return her calf. After days her lament grows silent.

The sensitivity of cows and bulls to blood kept Taleshis from participating in the bloodshed of infidels demanded by the Quran. The bloody revenge of Islam was strange to this nation until the Revolution of 1979, when Islamic culture began to penetrate the lives of Iranians. People called themselves Muslims, but their Zoroastrian background was still alive and separated them from the murder and revenge preached by Islam. Before the Revolution in 1979, I had never heard of anyone inciting others to take the blood of another as an act of revenge. Blood is a sign of tragedy and loss to Taleshis. Even cows and bulls, like their masters, are afraid of seeing or smelling blood. Even Chickens were never killed in a place where cows and bulls might catch the scent, because even the slightest drop of blood would cause the bulls to raise terrified voices of mourning and fear. This cry of the bulls would cause other bulls and cows to join them. Sometimes hundreds, even thousands of bulls and cows would rush from miles away to join in the crying and the mourning could continue for hours. Such an event would stop all activity in the village dead in its tracks because no Taleshi could risk losing sight of a family member among thousands of mourning animals.

I was amazed to discover that God used faithfulness in animals as an example to open the eyes of mankind. The Bible says that animals know their masters, but people do not know their Master: God. An event occurred in my life which caused me to understand the fullness of this message.

Animals know their masters well, which can serve the animal or the master either beneficially or to their detriment. For example, if a new master proves to be harsher than the previous owner, bulls and cows have been known to run away to return to more gentle conditions, and a bull who sings the praises of this master will win his favor.

I have a story to tell about a bull my father owned. The bull was three years old, and at that age a bull matures and begins the search for a mate. A bull's singing voice also matures at this age. A young bull is very territorial and combative, even toward humans, if they feel that a human male is approaching too closely to a cow that the bull has chosen for his mate. This has provoked many attacks on those who were unsuspecting, as my brother found to be painfully true.

One day our bull wandered from our land to the land where his mother came from. The bull was familiar with the man who had originally owned his mother. This man was very kind to animals and loved handsome bulls that had good voices. Our bull had a beautiful voice. All of the men in my family, including my father were very harsh, not only with people but also with their animals. Very few men in Taleshi families that I knew were as harsh as the men in my family. My brothers and I emulated our father, who was an angry and bitter man. We never welcomed openness, counseling or criticism. Women especially were prohibited from expressing their opinions in our presence. Even though we were able to feed our animals better than our neighbors were, it was evident that our bull preferred kindness over food.

We discovered our bull found a mate from that territory. My older sister, who lived in the area with her husband, saw the bull and passed the information to our family. My older brother got permission from my father to go to the village to retrieve the bull. My brother also had a romantic motive, and used the bull as an excuse to see his own girlfriend living in the village.

My father warned my brother that he must be careful when approaching the bull since he was now mature and had discovered a mate. When our bull saw my brother approaching, he sent a quick message through the movement of his body warning my brother to stay away or risk an attack. As my brother approached the bull, he noticed that his own girlfriend was watching him. My brother wanted to appear brave for her so he ignored the bull's warning.

The bull gored my brother. He was injured severely, but survived. My father was so enraged that he sold the bull to a butcher. The bull began to sing his beautiful bull song while tied in the front yard, waiting to leave for slaughter. His voice was so captivating that when my father's friend heard the song, he exclaimed, "You are not going to send this bull with a beautiful voice to the slaughter house, are you?" He tried to convince my father that the voice of the bull was like a treasure for the nation, and he must find a way to help the bull to live. He made fun of my father, saying, "You have also acted harshly toward us sometimes, so what should we do with you? Should we get rid of you? You have a beautiful voice too, and because of your beautiful voice we ignore your harshness." Then with a serious face, he said to my father, "The problem with this bull is that he is following the tradition of this family. He needs to follow my law." The man, a shepherd, convinced my father to give the bull to him in exchange for a cow and her calf, a generous trade. My father accepted the deal and the bull lived. The shepherd lived in a mountainous area to the west of our city, about 30 kilometers (19 miles) from our home, and managed to take the bull home with the help of friends and neighbors.

To "break" the angry bull the shepherd kept him under a yoke all day long for two months. He used him to plow the land every day. He also tied the bull in a very small place at night. Gradually, the bull lost muscle tone and became docile. My father was very harsh but his yoke was easier to bear than the new owner's yoke. Bulls love kind masters with an easy yoke. So one summer night, the bull became weary of the hard work and unkind master. He broke free of his rope and ran, returning to our home.

The end of rice sowing season ushers in summer. Taleshis typically move to the mountains during the summer months because the plains become unbearably hot and infested with flies and mosquitoes. Taleshis also take their livestock with them to spare them from the heat and insects. Even if they do not take their animals, the beasts will travel to the mountains, unguided, in order to escape the harsh weather and stinging insects. That summer, we had been unable to travel to the mountains.

I do not know why our bull rushed back to the plains during the summer: he certainly could not have known that we were home. In any case, he fled the cooler mountains and his new owner, and returned to the hot plains when the mosquitoes were swarming heavily. I suppose he preferred the Taleshi summer plains to the heavy yoke of his new owner.

Our bull arrived home in the middle of the night. He must have run all day. He would not have been able to complete the journey simply by walking. His new owner would have discovered that he was missing before he could have completed his 30 kilometer journey.

Normally bulls and cows do not sing at night, but when our bull arrived home he sang out, waking us all. My father, his two wives, my siblings and I jumped from our beds.

"It's our bull," my father cried. My mother confirmed, "Yes, it is he." My father took the lantern and walked toward the gate at the back of our house with two wives and twelve children following closely behind. As my father approached the gate, the bull shook his head and exhaled a quick and noisy breath to show he would not attack.

My father stretched his hand out over the gate and touched the bull's head saying "Oh, my brother," as a sign of his love for the beast. Then he opened the gate as the bull tapped it with his horns. We watched the bull walk through the yard. My father walked behind him, our mothers behind our father, and we children behind our mothers. We followed the bull into the front yard where he stopped beneath the trees. We were all standing around him and my father was rubbing the bull's body to welcome him. The bull brought his head down and touched his nose to the ground with a sniff to show my father that he was hungry and needed something to eat. My father fed him. It was then that our family witnessed what amounted to a tearful reconciliation between the bull and my father: This mirrored the reconciliation that occurs between Taleshis when they have wounded one another. This is something very deeply rooted in our culture, and filled with emotional symbolism with which I was so familiar. Sometimes I still cannot believe that a beast could touch a human heart so deeply but I know now that I witnessed God's word come true in that moment.

In Taleshi culture the time of reconciliation is when a victim willingly opens the door to the person who hurts him. Forgiveness is demonstrated by the preparation of a special meal for the offender. This show of love and tender-heartedness causes great remorse in the heart of the malefactor, and sorrow over one's wrongdoing is a tearful affair. These tears are accepted by a victim as a sign of sincere remorse and usually end in all parties crying and confessing their malevolence. This was exactly what the bull did with my father. While the bull was eating, we witnessed large tears flowing from his eyes. He was shaking his head continually and exhaling noisily expressing his apology and gentleness toward us. This display of emotion, coupled with his brave nighttime journey down from the mountains brought the entire family to tears. My father cried gently as he turned his face to my mother and said, "I should not have sold him. His return and kind attitude is a torture to my soul. I am so glad that I did not send him to the slaughter house."

I was reminded of the story of our bull once again in 1989, twenty five years later while in Turkey. The Iranian Christian preacher that I listened to that day referred to the following verses while teaching about Christ:

Come to me... For my yoke is easy and my burden is light.
(Matthew 11:28, 30)

The ox knows his master ... but...my people do not understand. (Isaiah 1:3)

In his message, the preacher raised his voice saying, "Even wild and weary bulls understand that kindness is good. They understand which yoke is an easy yoke and which one is not. They and their owners know each other very well. They recognize each other's voices. Oh God, do we need to learn from animals in this indifferent, disrespecting bloodthirsty world?"

While he spoke, tears flooded my eyes. After the sermon while church members ate, I was still crying. The preacher came to me with some other Christians to ask why I was crying. I said, "Well, I am a country boy. It is true. I know a wild bull who understood the easy yoke of his owner. I am also that wild bull who now understands what an easy yoke is." They praised God for not leaving a single nation without a witness for His glory. And I was amazed that how the words of the people, whom Islam calls infidels, were relevant to my life and I could identify myself with them.

Music and the Silent Cry of a Toddler

As a young boy, I was a bully. Among all my brothers I was the most religious but also the angriest. Strangely though, and contrary to my angry demeanor and hate-filled religious convictions, I was also a very sentimental and emotional boy who craved the loving touch of other people. A small touch and kindness were able to quickly dissolve any walls of anger and bitterness that I built daily around myself. My mother knew my emotional language well. More than any other person in our family she could always sustain and quiet me with her touch.

I was also, and still am, a great lover of music and singing. My love for music, even as a child, was profound. Many times, whenever I would hear music or someone singing, I cried silently so no one would hear me. Once as a toddler, riding on my older sister's back, I heard her singing a native country song as she walked through the garden. I remember resting my head on her shoulder and crying quietly. When my sister realized that I was crying, she put me down, held me in her arms, kissed me, and cried with me, saying, "Oh, my little baby, I am so sorry. I forgot that you are with me. You love it, don't you? I shouldn't have sung it."

My family was amazed and perplexed by my deep affection for music. My silent tears and ruminating at such an early age were somewhat confusing to my mother and siblings. I tend to attribute this emotion to the idea that, while safe in my mother's womb, I heard her and others singing or playing music while passing their days working in the fields, tending animals and preparing meals.

Music that Cries for Help and Unity

Taleshis are passionate about their traditional songs. Taleshi music is the nation's classical music. It represents the feelings and emotions of a hardworking and enduring people. The music of the nation has been suppressed however throughout the centuries by Islam. The old melodies that remain cry for help and unity. Even though Taleshis are now Muslims, they hold fast to their traditional culture, including music. Their music has helped them to live in unity despite the heavy pressures of Muslim rulers. I believe that many, if not most, Taleshis have become Muslims to placate Muslim rulers. If they profess even a nominal Muslim faith, they are able to protect their cultural values from complete eradication. This is what I witnessed after the Islamic revolution. The Taleshis were the last tribe to stand faithful to the kingdom of Persia and still many of them desire that Iran be led by a Persian king. A king who will protect their values and their culture under the democratic creeds proposed long, long ago by Cyrus and Darius, great Persian rulers. The Islamic Republic of Iran has been so cruel and so vicious to my people, yet, it has not been able to completely erase their cultural foundations.

Music also plays a vital role in the ritual of courtship. The Taleshi springs and summers are the seasons of poetic and romantic songs. All Taleshi songs are poems: this is a clue that the Taleshi people are an exceedingly romantic people by nature. Young men and women of Talesh normally fall in love in the spring and summer, as they seem to do everywhere else in the world. The fascinating, melodic beauty of spring and summer excites the senses after long, dreary winters. Eyes sparkle with youthful exuberance while the fresh scent of grass, flowers, hay and spring rain captures the fragrance of new life. It's an easy time to sing songs and write poems since there is fresh beauty everywhere.

Unfortunately Islam has limited the ability of lovers to express themselves to one another and has made it nearly impossible for young men and women to know each other before marriage. The degree to which relationships are limited prior to marriage depends largely on whether or not the country is ruled by fundamentalist Muslims or a nominal government body. Rigid Islamic rules make it extremely difficult, even dangerous, for a young woman to have a discussion or even be seen in public alone with a young man who is not a relative. A young woman seen in public with a man that is not her husband or relative can be tortured or stoned to death.

Taleshi girls and boys had far more freedom to speak to one another before the Revolution of Iran in 1979, despite the long presence of Islam in the region. Post-Islamic Revolution boys and girls were forced to resort to communicating through body language and eye contact. This was still risky because it broke Islamic law and could pose a serious threat, especially for girls. If a boy and a girl fell in love, the only way for them to see each other was through clandestine meetings, if they dared. Islam caused them to keep romantic conversations secret, even from their own families. Young people had to create opportunities and be creative in their excuses, as they sought to engage their beloved. They would seek each other out in work situations, work areas, or "chance" meetings in the street. Being sent to fetch water from the spring was a wonderful opportunity to meet someone, as was going out to collect wild berries. "Bumping" into someone and pretending to help gather their belongings from off the pavement was also a favorite and relatively safe sport for socializing between young men and women.

Many mothers within fundamentalist families realize the pressure placed on their children by Islam and are willing to arrange secret opportunities with friendly families in order to pave the way for their children's future marriages. This is generally not approved by the fathers of such families, and can prove to have dire consequences if a father becomes wise to the match-making schemes of his wife. The greatest punishment would be reserved for the daughter who would be considered defiled in the eyes of Islam and no longer fit for marriage, or even to live. Because of the fear created by Islam, a majority of marriages are arranged by parents. Young couples do not know each other before marriage.

If a boy and a girl fall in love with each other, it is typically expected for the girl to express her interest in the boy to her mother directly, or indirectly through one of her sisters or female relatives or friends. The mother will then speak to her husband to determine his response. Then she will convey the father's acceptance or rejection. Likewise, the young man will also make his feelings known to his mother, so she, in turn, can seek his father's approval. If the boy's father favors such a relationship, he will send two or more messengers to the girl's father to gain official permission for the young woman's hand in marriage. If the messengers receive a positive response, an engagement ceremony will be arranged at the young woman's family's home, where the dowry will also be established. Several months to a year later a marriage celebration is held at the boy's father's house. The girl is then taken to reside in the home of the boy's family. Marriage celebrations can last anywhere from three to seven days, depending on the boy's father. Musicians are hired to perform and sing at these celebrations if fundamentalist Muslims are not around.

It has not been easy for Islam to impose itself fully on the Iranian people because they are so strongly attached and deeply in love with their Persian heritage. People have learned to take back some of their traditions gradually, and secretly to preserve their cultural values, despite Islam's contrary demands. The Iranian people's powerful and subversive agendas have exhausted even the most zealous and cruel religious dictators and, in some cases, forced religious leaders to lighten the hand of oppression. This lightening was not out of compassion, but purely from the Iranians struggle for their cultural rights. Despite 1400 hundred years of Islamic influence in Persia, no religious leader has been able to stop Iranian people from enjoying music. At the beginning of the Revolution rigid Muslim judges ordered the Religious Guard to destroy musical instruments. Some were centuries old. However, despite these setbacks and attempts by Islamic extremists to squash music, the love of Iranians for their music persisted. This persistence exhausted even the grand leader, Ayatollah Khomeini, and as a result he finally had no choice but to remove some of the restrictions on music. Music is a life force for the Iranian people.

Miracle Child

I was born into a Muslim family; the fourth out of eight children from my mother. Before I was born, my parents lost a son. My brother was two years old when he died. My family told me he had been a bright boy and very sweet in his disposition. His death affected my parents in ways that only a parent who lost a child can begin to understand.

I was given his name when I was born. By the time of my birth my parents still had not reported my brother's death, for reasons known only to them. The government agency that handles such matters was never given the opportunity to cancel my brother's identification booklet. The booklet recorded a birth two years prior to mine but my parents decided to use it for me. They believed my birth was a miracle and God had given them another son to replace the child that had passed on. Before I was born my mother had already given birth to four children. She had a girl first, followed by a boy, then a girl, then a boy. When my mother was carrying me, after my brother's death, she was convinced I was a girl. My parents had perceived that my mother would continue to give birth in an alternating fashion, boy-girl-boy-girl: what a big surprise and blessing it was when I arrived as a boy. They believed that God had replaced the boy who died.

Child Prodigy

From the time I began to speak, my parents knew that I would be a fast learner. I was only four when my father enrolled me in primary school, but because of the identification booklet my parents had given to me I was admitted as a six year old. I attended school with my step-brother of six and a half years. Even though I was much younger, I managed my studies and exams far better than he. My step-brother was really struggling in school, so my father allowed him to quit after fifth grade. As for me, I delighted in the challenges and hard work required to complete homework. I enjoyed pursuing extra studies and would often sit studying late into the night aided by a lantern. I did not have a room or a study where I could tend to my work without disturbing others. I would work quietly in the same room where all of my siblings slept. Despite family and financial difficulties I earned high grades because of my hard work. This convinced my parents that I was truly a miracle sent by God to console them. It also led them to believe that I would grow up to be a godly man.

Many Muslims, including my parents, equate intelligence with godliness, because they know that a clever student will potentially be able to memorize the Quran (Koran), the holy book of Islam, and this is fundamental for the growth of a religious person. On the other hand, my parents were also keenly aware of my passion for music. This was confusing to them because they also knew that Islamic doctrine considers music to be evil. Why would Allah create a godly man to love that which Allah condemned? It seemed to contradict itself.

Because I was doing well in my studies my parents encouraged me to read and recite the Quran in Arabic, a foreign language to Iranians. By the time I was nine years old I was able to read the Quran in Arabic and recite its chapters from memory. People would frequently call on me to recite the Quran at their various religious events and ceremonies. This lifted me up in the eyes of people. Other boys were taunted by their parents for their inability to recite the Quran as I could. Every family desired to have at least one child who could recite the Quran over their grave after their deaths in order to subdue the torments of hell or to receive rewards for their souls from Allah on the Day of Judgment. The lack of a reciter of the Quran at a funeral gathering would bring humiliation to the family members of a deceased person, as no one could be found to recite the Quran for his/her sake. My ability to recite the Quran gained honor for my family members in every respect.

It seemed to be a misfortune that as I grew, my eyes became increasingly sensitive to sunlight. I was unable to open my eyes at all in the mornings until I had become properly adjusted to the daylight. My older brother would hold my hand while we made the hour long walk to school, and it wasn't until we arrived at school that I was able to open my eyes fully.

For the first nine years of my schooling, my family was unable to find a physician who could manage treatment for the problem of my eyes: there were no specialists in our city and travel costs were prohibitive. Fortunately, by the time I reached tenth grade, I was able to save enough money from jobs I worked in weekends and during holidays to pay for a doctor who could prescribe the proper optical prescription for my condition.

Two Families

According to Islam, a man can legally marry up to four wives and have as many concubines as he likes. The practice of keeping concubines was not popular in our town, and very few Taleshi men practiced polygamy, but my father had two wives and managed to father 12 children between them. My father was married to my mother until three years before I was born. He then took another girl as his second wife. My mother could not protest my father's decision to bring a second wife into our family.

My father was not a religious man but he considered himself to be a Sunni. His wives were both Shiites. Traditionally, religious Muslims marry people from their own sect, but because my father was not fundamentally religious he married whomever he pleased. The fact that Shiites were dominant in our region very likely played a key role in the fact that my father was not particular about what religious sect his wives came from. My mother seemed to be more religious than my father but she could still pass for a nominal and superstitious Muslim; they did not know Islam and were unable to understand Islamic fundamentalism.

There were two languages spoken in our home. My father, stepmother and all children of the family spoke to each other in Taleshi, but my father and my mother's children all spoke to my mother in Azeri, the language of my mother's people, the Azerbaijanis. My mother did not know Taleshi when she married my father, but he spoke Azeri and was able to communicate with her in her language. It kept the language in the family. I didn't learn Persian (Farsi), the official language of Iran until I started school. This is often one of the biggest surprises for people, because they do not realize Iran has many different languages.

Country Living

I grew up in a mud-wood, two-room house that I shared with eleven brothers and sisters and three parents. The two rooms we shared also connected to something like a veranda. There was a store room attached to the house with a summer room above it, only much more primitive. We were forced to sleep there whenever the humid summer months became overbearing. We would all fifteen of us sleep on the floor, covered with mosquito nets. Traditional Taleshi homes were made of timber and mud mixed with hay, and the poorest families would have to cover their roofs with rice straw, which is the cheapest material available. The rich and middle class families covered the roofs of their houses with wooden sheeting, tiles and sheet-metal. Storms would often blow away the hay with which my father thatched our roof, and rain would come pouring down into our house. Our financial difficulties prevented my father from ever fixing our roof properly. On rainy days we placed all our pots and bowls under the leaking ceiling to keep the rooms as dry as we could.

Our family owned a small rice farm which did not have good soil and, sadly, never produced enough to feed us. In order to meet our most basic provisions, my mother, step-mother and older sisters were forced to work on other farms. Having enough food for our family was always a struggle. We often ate rice three times a day. With the rice was a side dish that could consist of walnut, yogurt, milk, butter, cheese, egg, vegetable, jam or both home-grown and wild herbs. Sometimes we could afford to have more side dishes with our rice. Rarely could we eat chicken or meat or fish with our rice. Our parents preferred to keep them for the feast days or when we had visitors.

During the seasons of sowing and harvesting crops every family member was expected to work and help. While the adults were out working in the fields the children would gather firewood, prepare meals for the entire family, and haul water from neighborhood springs or wells. Sometimes we would even take wares to market to sell or trade so we could buy bread and other staples. I do remember preparing and baking the traditional Taleshi flat bread in a clay oven when I was a very young child.

The rice harvest arrives at the end of summer, and the new rice is eaten in celebration with neighbors and friends. A colorful table is prepared with the harvested rice and other wonderful and delicious foods. All of the men ate together in one room and the ladies in another, except when all male and females are close family relatives. In this case, they all have their meal together. The traditional way to begin such a celebration is for the father of the family to touch the cooked new rice and begin eating. This signals the commencement of the festivities wherein all those in attendance are able to partake.

When everyone has eaten his fill, each person is expected to leave just a spoonful of food on their plate, signifying a blessing on the family for abundance, and more rice than is even needed for the entire year. Many people hold their new rice celebrations in the fall. Some very rich families will wait until winter to celebrate the late summer harvest as a sign of the abundance in their lives. But families like mine, who could not afford to wait for the food, held their celebration in the last month of summer after the harvest. We children were filled with excitement during the rice feasts because we could eat plenty.

For centuries Taleshis would move to their mountain homes to wait out the extremely humid and mosquito-infested summer months from the time the rice was planted until harvest. The weather was cool and pleasant in the mountains; no bugs, no humidity, only sweet, cool breezes. Taking part in the mountain retreats was wonderful and sometimes inspirational. While my father was alive we rarely made the trip. It was only after his death that my family was able to save enough money to enjoy those wonderful mountain retreats.

Life with Father

My father, unlike Taleshi men, and his hard-working wives and children, was not a working person. He felt that work was only for women and children. He was a dictator and no one in our home dared to question him. His relationship with the family was like the relationship of a master to his slaves. If he raised his voice we all had to stand at attention. His best moments were when he had money in his pocket and could go to the bazaar (market) to spend time with other men like himself. He spent most of his time in tea houses with other men and spent our family's money in the lotto. He did not disguise his dislike for the feudal class which earned him respect among his peers. He was also notorious for his fearsome reputation and even his closest friends were very careful in his company. They knew he could easily turn on them with one wrong word. He loved to have friends but his nature prevented him from maintaining any good and lasting relationships. Without warning he could become extremely violent toward any who spoke against him, and it was equally strange and surprising to see him become gentle when someone praised him. He loved to be praised but was not able to ever tolerate any criticism or opposition. This dualistic personality made him an easy and predictable target for those ready to take advantage of him. The cleverest deceivers were able to empty my father's pocket with the slightest praise. My father's pride ruled him but it also eventually ruined him. His life was a continual failure because of his confused and complicated mind.

With no talent for making money and unable to save, my father lived one day at a time, too busy to be concerned about his and his family's future. He considered manual labor a disgrace, and quickly squandered the money his family earned by working on other farms. My grandfather and his brothers were rich and prestigious people among the community. My father received a healthy inheritance after the death of my grandfather but spent it all in a very short time. All that remained was shallow and superficial family prestige.

The village community treated my father as an elder because of the legacy that his family left him. My father however did not possess the values of prevalent Taleshi style eldership nor did he desire them. My father believed that an elder of the community should not work. "Working for others reduces the authority of eldership", he believed. "A boss must always be boss." These were not the attitudes of all Taleshi men. Most Taleshi people were hardworking farmers and for the sake of their families they preferred helping their families to any kind of eldership. For this reason they struggled through long days and long nights.

My father's hobbies were chickens and an orchard. He loved to have every kind of chicken in the yard, which could be costly whenever diseases were introduced into the yard by other chickens. He also collected all kinds of fruit plants from everywhere and planted them in our orchard. But he was only a collector, leaving the care of the chickens and the orchard to the family. If we lost a chicken to a fox or a jackal or a plant was broken by an animal then it was woe to the family. His graceless attitudes caused us to take refuge in lying sometimes and rescue ourselves from his attacks.

One day on a school holiday, we (three brothers) were asked to look after the house and watch our birds. We lost several of our ducks to a fox that day. We knew that our father would punish us harshly. We were trying to find a way to escape his punishment. Our plan worked. I was instructed by my older brother to take the blame and sit by the main road a hundred yards far from our house. I was to cry hard as soon as I saw our father coming from the bazar. My cry we thought may scare him and soften his heart toward us. Our middle brother took the responsibility to hide outside the house and watch our father's reaction and report it to the older brother. If he was furious then my brothers could run away and hide. Long story short I saw my father coming from a mile away. I started to cry naturally because of my fear. When father got closer to me I sobbed so hard I almost fainted. This scared my father to death, thinking that something really horrible may have happened to the family. He was nervous and continually asked what happened, but I could not speak clearly because of my sobbing. Eventually I was able to inform him that a fox had left a few of our ducks dead in the orchard and taken others. He sighed a breath of relief when he heard this and said something unbelievable: "For the death of a few birds you are terrified and terrifying me! I don't care about them." He then lifted up me from the dust and walked me to the house. When the middle brother saw him he also started to cry. Then my father left to calm him down. As he was talking to my middle brother I rushed home and gave the good news to the older brothers that our father was not angry. The older brother also started to cry when he saw father. His words to the older brother were nice also. We were happy to escape his punishment that day. We kept that day secret until our father's death. After that, it became a source of laughter in the family.

My father was not religious nor was he against religion, but he did not like religious clerics (*mullahs*). He believed they talked about moral standards that they themselves were unable to follow. Unlike many Taleshis, he did not like the ruling king, because the middle class and poor were unable to stand for their rights against the rich. He was openly critical of the mullahs because mullahs were not in power in that time, but he refrained from openly criticizing the king for fear of endangering his own life.

My father had his own ideas. According to my father, women needed no education, and he did not like the idea of freedom for women, a belief which placed him in direct opposition to the king of Iran. Though he was a dictator to us and especially to his wives, he also knew that a wife could take her husband to a court for his unjust treatments. For this reason, we sometimes saw fear in his face when he was harsh. Strangely, my father would never tolerate even the slightest injustice toward his family from others, all the while inflicting extremely harsh treatment on us. And true to his bizarre inconsistencies and erratic behavior my father was still always very generous to the needy.

Home Sweet Home

I never heard of a man with more than one wife also having a peaceful home. The two mothers in our home always worked very hard, but were never happy to share life with each other. Anytime they had an opportunity to ignore one another or one another's children they would do it. This subversive behavior was kept secret from my father, who would never tolerate discord between the two wives and their children. If my father discovered such discrimination he would make their lives very difficult. Sometimes problems would escalate between the two women to such a degree that my father's reactions were treated with indifference. Eventually, it seemed that my mother and stepmother had given up any hope concerning their futures and personal desires. So my father's rebukes soon became commonplace and irrelevant to them, allowing them to practice their pettiness toward each other more openly as the years passed. I never heard them express any wishes for themselves or their futures, but only that their children would grow safely and that they would each find their way to a good future that was different from the lives they were living. They did and were ready to do everything for their children in order to see them moving ahead.

The life for the girls of our family was not promising at all. They were pressured by my father to marry men whom they did not like. Girls got married at a young age since my father was able to receive their dowries. However was in no hurry for his sons to marry, because he had to pay a dowry.

Aim High

Every day was a struggle for my family. My father's expectation for his sons was to graduate from ninth grade, find a job and make money so he could continue his leisurely lifestyle. I worked hard to earn money to bribe him to allow me to continue my schooling. It was my clever capitalist mentality that convinced my father that I could be both a good student and an excellent money maker. When I received good marks I would spread the news among our family and the community in order to bring honor to my father and draw his attention to me. Bringing honor to my father was another way of making him happy. I labored very hard under the certainty that a higher education would guarantee a good job with substantial income, and that I would also be elevating myself socially and politically. My desire was to make a better life for my family.

The one thing that always threatened the study of many native Taleshi children was the high cost of education and the inability of families to pay for it. Because of these obstacles, many Taleshis were satisfied if their children learned only the basics of reading and writing. Students who pursued higher education had to find a way to earn enough income to finance their education and also to help their families. This measure was taken to ensure that a student remained in his parents' favor; otherwise the student might be forced to return home to continue laboring.

Lifestyle differences between the city and villages also created obstacles for us country students to continue school. Wealthy urban citizens who were not natives, including many teachers and students, viewed villagers as less civilized or retarded. Some teachers would taunt lazy students from the city, calling them villagers. This kind of discrimination was common. If a student struggled, people would say, "Are you a villager? Have you come from a mountain?" Even though many of us were excellent students, some teachers were convinced that we would not succeed.

It was common for individuals from rural areas to feel the sting of discrimination in the city. I believe that the disdain that many city dwellers poured on country people caused them to isolate themselves from city life. This certainly helped to perpetuate the lack of education in villages and agricultural communities. Some students would go so far as to avoid associating with their families who would sometimes go to the city to shop, all for the sake of appearing civilized.

I would often ask myself, "If I finish school and live in the city, will I be able to marry a girl from the city and still retain my family ties? Would my spouse tolerate the life that my siblings and parents lived, and would she be interested in knowing them?" It was difficult to believe that this could ever be a reality, so I did everything in my power to avoid confronting that issue. I decided that I would wait until I graduated to concern myself with relationships, even though I wanted so much to be married. I was especially careful to avoid city girls because I knew that I would have to navigate social obstacles. There were many times when I responded negatively toward girls who I really liked, just to avoid having to deal with the possibility that they might reject my family, a possibility that was unbearable to me.

One day in the university library I saw the most beautiful girl I had ever seen in my life. I couldn't take my eyes off her. She was so lovely and I couldn't believe that she was looking at me. Because she didn't look away when our eyes met, I knew that she wanted to talk to me. The thought of such a beauty desiring my attention was captivating and exciting. I wanted so much to know her but everything about her told me that she was not only a city girl, but she was from an affluent family. I couldn't tear my thoughts away from my family, and I couldn't escape the fact that there were too many factors working against any hope for me ever being with her.

This attitude is difficult for many contemporary Westerners to understand—because they believe that social barriers are not barriers at all—but in the Middle East these are walls that are virtually insurmountable. I decided to ignore the lady. My lack of attention to her did not discourage her. One day she just sat right down next to me in the library and asked me the time. I thought it would be fun to tease her and make fun of her so I gently took her hand and read the time from the watch on her wrist. She was so embarrassed she quickly gathered her belongings to leave but as she left I saw love in her eyes. Watching her leave was the hardest thing because parts of my heart had always been filled with poetry and romance and love and I wanted to share it all with her and learn from her.

The challenges for country boys were great. I could not simply forget my past and discard my family for the sake of marriage. I couldn't forget my family's hard work, love and encouragement. I reminded myself that I needed to appreciate their sacrifices instead of concerning myself with the disadvantages of having been born a country boy.

After the Revolution in 1979 I married a girl from the city. We were both revolutionaries. I was hoping that the spirit of the so-called borderless Revolution would remove the existing city-country barriers and unite us as two human beings. Instead, the differences and barriers ran very deep and have always been trying to tear us apart. Similar cultural problems also arose in my political life with my colleagues after the Revolution.

Some city revolutionaries who called themselves freedom supporters, started to mistreat or mock those of us who were from villages. They said to the public, "Look at the riders of donkeys who aim to lead a nation." They meant that only their seemingly civilized compatriots, those who rode horses, would be able to run the country. It was painful to endure such discrimination at the time, but that experience brought joy to me years later when I read the story of the King of kings (Revelation 19:16) who entered Jerusalem on a humble donkey (Matthew 21:5; Zachariah 9:9) and did not worry what those who claimed to be civilized thought.

As a student I worked hard to rescue myself from the village and its unbearable lifestyle, and from every other obstacle that I felt was hindering my progress. To help support schooling costs as well as some family expenses, my step-brother and I collected firewood to sell during those days we were not in school. We did this when it was not sowing or harvest time.

At these times no member of the family would have free time for anything other than farming. We spent hours and hours in a nearby forest. I would climb the trees, cutting the thicker branches for charcoal and thinner branches for fire wood. We gathered as much as we could carry on our backs and also on our donkey.

Our enterprising activities in the forest helped me to become a very skillful tree climber. I always stood upright, high in the trees on my bare feet, and fearlessly cut the branches with a sharp ax. My stepbrother was not good at climbing the trees; he preferred to do the ground work. He would cut the fallen branches into short pieces so that we could carry them. We would take them home and lay the thicker pieces in a kiln in our yard for producing charcoal, and sell the thinner branches for firewood. The money we made from selling charcoal was much better than what we made from selling firewood, because we sold the coal directly to businessmen, while the firewood was sold to individuals in the city. But we worked hard to do both because we needed every bit of income. We also had to prove to our father that we were hard-working children who did not want to burden the family. Despite our constant work, I was still able to maintain good grades in school.

My mother and siblings always supported my desire for a higher education. In my father's absence, they encouraged me to achieve my educational goals. Without their moral support and help, I would not have been able to survive my father's opposition. Sometimes I would think, "If my father tried to prevent me from going to school, I would not obey him no matter what the cost." As the years passed, my father saw my success and eased his pressure on me to retreat from my studies.

2

Practicing Islam

Nominalism

In the not so distant past, the religious climate of Iran separated religion and politics, and people were encouraged to become religious nominalists. The last king of Iran, Mohammad Reza Shah, influenced by his father, understood that Persians would not survive if they did not distance their political philosophy from the rigid authoritarianism of Islam. History has proven that the Shah's reign over Persia was a pinnacle of freedom in comparison to other Muslim kingdoms since the dominance of Islam. The Shah was wise to the fact that Islam is a political religion which desires to dominate every aspect of the lives of its followers, both political and private. He claimed to be a good Muslim but in his practical life he distanced himself from Islam and from many religious leaders, and showed a more pro-western attitude. The power of Islam makes it virtually impossible for Muslims to distance themselves from the politico-religious influence of Islam. Muslims are expected to surrender even the most mundane aspects of their lives, and resistance is costly.

Prior to the 1979 Revolution religious fundamentalism was not present in northern Iran. People readily called themselves Muslims but did not practice according to Islamic expectations. Some Islamic holy days were observed by some but most were accustomed to nationalism. They were more inclined to recognize national holidays than religious ones. The popular confession of the majority of people around the Caspian Sea was, "God, King and the Motherland." Even after the Revolution, when I helped other revolutionaries deliver food and household necessities to needy families, many recipients expressed their gratitude by exclaiming "Long live the King". We had made it known that the gifts were from the religious leaders, or the mullahs, but they refused to accept that anyone but the Shah was providing for them. They knew that the king had been deposed and had fled the country but they insisted that the Shah had left these gifts for his countrymen. The idea of a government being generous was unfathomable. Only kings were generous. We did not deal harshly with citizens who denied the benevolence of the new government because the theocracy of Islam had not yet fully taken hold in Iran.

Taleshis were unwilling to accept the idea of Iran without a king. The royal heritage of Persia is ancient and dates back thousands of years. It is a great source of pride for Iranians, evidenced even today in their reverence for King Cyrus and King Darius. Even the most brutal Saudi Arabian invaders could not establish the demands of their prophet Muhammad by erasing the kingdom mind-set of Iranians. Iranians, excluding Islamic zealots, would love to return to the days of glory which they associate with the reign of Persian kings 2500 ago, and thereby regain their nation's honor.

Raising Muslims

Taleshi children were supposed to follow the faith of their father so I submerged myself in religious activities. I sang lamentations in mosques with a mournful voice, leading people to mourn and weep for ancient Shiite Arabian martyrs.

I do not know why I chose to follow my mother's sect (Shi'a) rather than my father's (Sunni) because I, like my parents, didn't know the difference between the two. Perhaps it was because my father was not interested in practicing religion as outwardly as my mother. I suppose I was drawn by my mother's religiosity and less interested in my father's indifference to religion. My father's interest in Islam was strictly limited to whatever might gain him honor among his peers, which is the case with many other Muslim parents. A child who could recite the Quran, as I could, is revered by both Sunnis and Shiites. It was for this reason that, although I did not follow my father's religious sect, he never discouraged me. It was very much to his advantage to be the father of the most religious child in our village.

Taleshi parents are not all devout Muslims, but are enslaved by doctrines causing them to desire religious children. Muslims have been taught that all righteous and unrighteous Muslims will be gathered around hell first,[1] and if their good deeds outweigh their bad deeds they are taken to paradise by Allah. Muslims consider that Allah looks favorably upon prayers for the dead. The deceased person for whom prayers and the Quran are recited finds favored in Allah's sight and may gain entry to the bliss of paradise.

My parents encouraged this philosophy from the time I could read and recite the Quran in Arabic. This created a deep desire in me for religious matters, even though I did not understand Arabic. My ability to memorize the Quran and recite it in religious gatherings made me famous at a young age. I was strongly attached to the mosques in the area. People revered my religious zeal.

Islam, I was aware, aimed to first rid the world of all other religions but I did not know how this would happen. Our religious exercises at that time were a bit different from what is now practiced under the rule of the Islamic Republic of Iran. We were Muslims by name but Zoroastrians (the religion of Persians before Islam) in practice. We were not conscious of the fact however. Zoroastrianism does not believe in imposing religion on others and does not believe in evangelism. A Zoroastrian believes that an individual will find his way to

---

1   Q19:68-72..

31

Zoroastrianism by building his life on good thoughts, words and deeds, and especially through doing good deeds for others. It is like all other man-made religions based on works rather than on the wonderful unmerited grace given by Jesus Christ.

I believed that my zealous religious practices would increase my ability to rely on God and I hoped to receive from Allah all the strength needed to reach my spiritual and worldly goals. All I knew of Islam was superstition, ceremony, and traditional daily practices. Knowing such things made me good enough to be called a religious person in the eyes of non-practicing Muslims. In reality however, they were hollow and meaningless because I was never connected to the One True God by any of these outward acts of self-righteousness.

I had to pray five times a day in Arabic; one must not pray to Allah in one's mother tongue. Allah will only accept prayers in Arabic, the words which Muhammad, the prophet of Islam, determined for Muslims to recite five times a day. Most Taleshi villagers could not pray in Arabic, but this is the only way a person was allowed to stand for prayer in Islam. Many people still did not know how to pray after thirteen hundred years of Islamic rule in Iran and the pressure of Muslim leaders on Iranians to learn Arabic. This had a great deal to do with the fact that our Taleshi forefathers were very disinterested in Islam; this legacy remains true even today.

God Hears

For Taleshis the most practical way of talking to God has always been through sighs and groans expressed in the native language. These expressions to God stem from their deep spiritual longings that cannot be uttered in words. This type of prayer is unconvincing to Allah, the god of Islam who ignores other languages. However these heart-felt prayers had a great impact on me. They were the natural cries of the heart and Taleshis knew God could not ignore deep crying from one's soul. Taleshi prayers were in stark contrast to Islam's rituals.

It is no surprise to me that Taleshis would not prefer the cold meaningless redundancy of Muslim prayers to the cries of the soul to a God who has compassion for tears and contrite hearts.

By the age of nine I had learned the Islamic prayers and was able to pray in Arabic. However, the soulful sighs and groans of the prayers of people in their own language seemed to me more poetic, touching, and attractive. This led me to be interested in the aesthetic aspect of spiritual life practiced by some of my fellow citizens. I fell in love with traditional Persian ascetic poetry: the desires of a simple life that is focused overridingly on discovering God in this world, to know and be known personally by God, and to be absorbed in Him. I believe this is a testimony that the God of Abraham, Isaac and Jacob has left among Iranians in order to lead them to Jesus Christ.

I think back now and remember that some of my most lucid moments of meditation with God came when I was doing my schoolwork under the trees in my father's orchard. My mind was always working out ways in which I could attain my personal goals for financial and educational success. Because my family's financial situation was always uncertain it seemed to me that my goals were unattainable. This caused me to rely on God more and more, seeking His supernatural intervention in my life. There in my father's orchard I would express my needs and the deepest desires through the sighs and groans of the soul, much like those prayerful expressions I share with the Lord Jesus today.

It is interesting to me that what my culture taught me as a child, which I later discarded as a Muslim, has come full circle in my life as my Gracious Heavenly Father works through me in prayer. Though I had no knowledge of God, those moments with Him convinced me that God was good and all good things were His attributes and must have come from Him.

33

Ignorance Isn't Bliss

As a Muslim I was taught that in order to attract God's attention, we must read the Quran in Arabic, even though we could not understand what we were reading. I neither knew the meaning of the verses of the Quran, nor anything about Muhammad, the prophet of Islam or his successors. My parents had no knowledge of Islam: they blindly inherited their beliefs from their forefathers who had been forced to follow Islam. Our parents were expected to pass the legacy of Islam to their children for future generations and no one was allowed to question that legacy. To be a Sunni or a Shiite had become nothing more than a family tradition rather than a religion of choice. Fortunately, people from both sects in Talesh enjoyed peaceful relationships with each other. Prior to the Islamic Revolution I had never experienced any religious fighting among the followers of these two sects in my hometown. It was not until after the 1979 Revolution that religious beliefs among Taleshis took on a political character, and Shiite leaders, becoming proud of their majority status, began to discriminate against the Sunni minority.

Since childhood, we had continually heard verses from the Quran translated into Persian, which stated that Jews and Christians were unclean.[2] It was common to humiliate someone during an argument by calling that person the son of a Jew or a Christian. This was also the attitude of radical Muslim leaders who spread this hatred among the people. They desired to prepare an atmosphere for discrimination and ethnic and religious cleansing. To the shame of Iranians and the cultural tolerance inherited from the ancient kings, Cyrus and Darius, this attitude of discrimination is now widespread throughout all of Iran. The war between the Persian culture and Islam has dominated Iran since the invasion and occupation of Arabian Muslims (633-656 AD). There were many times throughout history when the struggle for power between Persia and Islam illustrated the strength of one over

2   Q9:28.

the other. However, Iranians were never able to completely rid themselves of the Saudis' hostile culture because of their fearful and sometimes blind obedience to Islam. Belief systems are the strongest and most influential factors that shape the values of a culture. Iranians once tolerated all beliefs. Now it is hard for them to believe that an Iranian can be a Jew or a Christian or a Zoroastrian, or indeed any other religion.

I never knew anything about Christianity, Judaism, or any religions beyond Islam and Zoroastrianism because Islamic religious leaders teach that Islam is the final and perfect religion brought to finish the work of God on earth. It was not for us to question whether a religion or idea could be superior to Islam so there was no need to read about other belief systems. The call of a Muslim is one of blind obedience. Death is the penalty for believing the superiority of any other book over the Quran. Islam teaches that no one is able to understand the words of a transcendent Allah[3], and for an ignorant mortal to presume to compare the words of "Allah" to another religion is an affront to Islam and worthy of the wrath of man and Allah.

Iranian Poets Concur

I certainly did not know many things about Jesus Christ. All I ever heard from clerics about Jesus was that He was a good prophet but for Jews only. From a purely political standpoint, committed Muslims believe that Jesus' success was impeded because of His apparent inability to compel the entire nation of Israel to follow Him. Also they believe Muhammad was sent after Jesus to establish Islam and finish the work Jesus left incomplete. However this is not the view commonly held by Persian poets, many of whom wrote of a relationship with Jesus Christ.

Mawlana Rumi, a 13th century AD philosopher and poet, said, "Die to self at the feet of Jesus, as I died to myself fully". Hafez, another 14th century AD great Iranian lyric poet, said, "The

---

3   Q3:7; 7:188.

load of pain that was torturing us, God sent Jesus to us to rid us of this pain and took Him back again". Sa'di, another 13th century AD poet quoted the words of the gospel of Christ in a poem saying, "If the world tortures one member of a body, there will not be peace in other members of the body." Their personal philosophies correspond remarkably to Christ's teachings, the Gospel of Christ and Christianity.

I became very much interested in Persian poetry from ninth grade and involved myself in writing my own poems and reciting the poems of others. I discovered the humble approaches of these great poets to Jesus Christ and was amazed. I was not able to ask why they did not speak about Muhammad in a similar manner.

I believe the writings of these men are a testimony of God's plan for Iranians. He allowed the name of Christ to be magnified in Persian poetry so that Iranians, like me, might see the excellence of Christ without first opening a Bible. By reading the Bible they would be amazed how God paved the ground for them to unite with Him.

Childhood Prophecy

One day in seventh grade our teacher dismissed us for an hour onto the playground for recess. Seven boys, including myself, got together, wondering what to play. One of the boys said he knew a game. He tore a piece of paper from his notebook and divided it into seven pieces. He then proceeded to write something on each piece of paper without showing it to us. He folded up each piece of paper into a tiny square and mixed them up and said, "Each person must take only one ballot and open it in turn. Each ballot will show the future of the person who carries it."

After we each took a ballot we playfully and excitedly argued about who would open their ballot first. I was the seventh and last boy to open his ballot. What was written on each ballot referred to various kinds of worldly jobs or positions such as a teacher, an army officer, a mayor, a doctor, or an engineer. I held the last ballot unopened in my hands, obviously not knowing its content. Like the other students, I was having fun, trying to guess what my future would hold. Expecting my ballot to hold some noble prophecy, I opened it and all at once my lighthearted expectations were shattered. It said, "You will become a Christian in the future." The words on the ballot were a shocking blow. All of the boys burst into laughter, mocking and teasing me. Suddenly I became strangely paranoid thinking that this boy must be my enemy. The humiliation was unbearable because I was a religious Muslim. I felt as though I was being accused of something terrible: Christians were unheard of in our school and region. The pressure of the moment was tremendous. I felt trapped and threatened. I thought to myself "How dare someone call me a Christian?" My thoughts turned to violence and revenge. I was angry and wanted to kill the boy who wrote the ballots. I began beating him and shouting "Why did you write such a disgusting thing for me?"

As I continued to beat my classmate he cried out in terror and fear and tried to desperately shield himself from the blows laid on him. He cried, "I did not write it for you. You and the others saw that I folded the ballots very well, mixed them very well in front of your eyes, and no one was able to distinguish them from each other, or who was going to take which ballot. I swear to God that I did not know who was going to take it. I could have picked it. We were just playing a game. No other student put it in your hand. We all picked ours before you, and you were the last one with the last ballot. You have no right to blame me."

I realized that he was right. I had taken the ballot myself and I had fought for the right to be the last boy to take the final ballot. I stopped beating my classmate but my anger and embarrassment forced me to leave the group. I retreated to a quiet place in a corner, crying out to God and demanding to know why He would allow such a thing to happen to me. While groaning, I also asked myself a question, "Why is it so hard for a Muslim to become a follower of Jesus Christ? If it was not, then I would have fun in playing with my friends but not grief."

Twenty years later, after my walk with Christ began, I still remembered that game and realized it was not my classmate or Allah who caused me so much personal grief. It was the real God, who had allowed that incident to occur. God demonstrated His providence through that incidence in my life. I realized His plan for me had been laid out and no one was able to demolish it. I believe He was leaving a trail of memories for me to look back on and ponder, to soften my heart and reconcile me to Him. Through no worth of my own, God had reached into my life from eternity and left tokens of His grace so that I might become a trophy of His grace.

Searching for God

It was ninth grade when I found my interest in Persian poetry. I had an interest in classical poems which taught a kind of ascetic philosophy called Erfan. Some Iranian poets encourage meditation on the original condition of man's relationship with God prior to his fall. This method of exploring thoughts and feelings through a simple lifestyle was meant to bring man closer to God. The Erfan encourages a life of deprivation and isolation and encourages a critical mind-set toward secular and religious leaders who promote religiosity and hypocrisy. The Erfan encourages people to attain a life of purity and love. It also condemns the killing of all life forms, even an ant.

Some poets describe the cause of humanity's despair as having been brought about by man's separation from God. This is the cause of all suffering and pain. In Iran people esteem such poets as those who are able to reach God because they have preferred a simple life. The reason that Jesus is revered in Iranian poetic culture is because of His simplicity and His sacrificial love. Jesus Christ has served as the greatest of all models of inspiration of this ascetic style of poetry. Why? He did not own anything, not even a pillow, while He was in this world. This embodies humility and unconditional love in its purest form. This is yet another example of how God has left His witness in the culture of those who were not searching for Him. God allowed Himself to be found by those who had not heard His gospel and yet, through cultural means, Persians were able to see the beauty and value of Christ through their poetry.

As a young man I loved the simplicity of these poets' lives. I wished to be wise and lead a simple life as they did. I desired to be unaffected by the pain, heartache, and struggles of life. Of course, as I have continued in my walk with Christ, I see that asceticism and isolation are not the answers, that the pain and suffering I endure with Christ make me more like Him in respecting and loving others.

Deep in my heart I longed to leave the confines of my surroundings and travel across the world. I wanted to know God in the context of the world. Somehow I imagined that as my horizons expanded so would the simplicity and purity of my relationship with God. I wanted to enroll in a different high school where I could major in Persian literature and poetry, paving the ground in myself for more investigation in the future and establishing myself as a noble spiritual man in Erfan. My family's financial constraints prevented me from making such a move. Ultimately, I limited myself to desires of reaching out into the world and discover the spirituality that I felt I had lost somewhere. It was a very vague thing that I was searching for, something intangible which I could not flesh out in my thoughts. Of course I had no clue that I was going to find The Way. It wasn't going to come to me as I imagined it would.

My family life, along with its particular struggles, did not allow me any extra time to pursue Erfan or to study the lives and philosophies of the ancient poets in any depth. Everyone in my family, except my father, was busy working hard just to survive. I was very concerned that the harshness of my reality would force me to quit school so I worked even harder to make money for the sake of paying tuition and supplies. As I was struggling to make ends meet the desire to pursue Erfan was growing stronger. I see now that the difficulties and struggles of my life were a complement to the lifestyle of self-denial that was the mark of Erfan.

One can learn many lessons from a harsh life. In my spare time, I spent countless nights staring at heaven and expressing my heart to a God that I did not yet know. I hoped to one day experience what I instinctively knew would be peace through the knowledge of God in my heart. I did not yet have enough knowledge of Islam to be able to understand whether the desires of my heart were in line with Islam's doctrine, but I was thinking in my heart that I could go to God, that I could reach Him if I tried hard. I didn't know that my sin created a wall between me and God and separated me from Him. Nor did I know that I was unable to bring this wall down and reach God; only God could shatter this wall and reach me. All of my understanding of God was what my imagination had concocted. I thought that if I tried my best He would help me to reach to Him. Of course any time I thought about barriers I felt helpless. I lifted my eyes and heart to Heaven, seeking help from the Creator whose name was still unknown to me.

Throughout my life, since ninth grade and until I believed in Jesus Christ, I experienced a never changing dream: I was flying through the sky, and an unknown voice always warned me "Do not look down to earth. Look at heaven always or you will fall and die." In my dream if I did look down it was horrifying experience. I would begin dropping to earth like a stone faster and faster until I reached a terrifying speed that finally woke me up. When I dreamt again sometimes I remembered the consequence of looking down. I was obedient to that voice and kept my face toward heaven and enjoyed the peace of flying. Years later, in the early days of my Christian life in Turkey, the words of the voice in my dream presented itself

40

in a Turkish Christian: *Yere bakan dushar, goge bakan yashar,* which means, "Anyone who looks at earth will fall down, but the one who looks at heaven will live." He recited this Turkish poetic wisdom to me when he heard about the bitterness in my life. I was shocked and amazed. He shook his head in opposition to the unfriendly approaches of this world. With amazement I asked him, "What does this poem mean?" He responded, "The prince of this world is Satan, but the Prince of Heaven is Jesus Christ. If we put our trust in Him who is in Heaven, we will not fall into the chains of Satan." His words made we wonder for years whether there was supernatural mouth speaking to me. I found that my dream was fulfilled by the intervention of Jesus Christ in my life. Those who fix their eyes on heavenly things will soar with Christ as the eagles but those who cast their eyes upon the earth and its desires will fall and die eternally.

3

Life in Tehran

Radio and television influenced and dramatically shaped the desires and demands of Iran's children. As we grew up they were broadcasting the western lifestyle of the 1970's. By tenth grade I was able to see the cultural difference between East and West. This was a far cry from reading about it and discussing it with my schoolmates. We had envisioned a prosperous West but it was beyond our imaginations. The freedom Westerners enjoyed might as well have been happening on another planet because it was so far from the lives my classmates and I lived. The Revolution had not yet happened in Iran but we were still captive to the strict demands of Islam. Speaking out against Islam was taboo and costly. We witnessed the resistance of committed Muslims to the impact of Western culture and its clothing styles in particular on us younger generations. I sometimes felt embarrassed for attaching myself so strongly to Islam and depriving myself of the freedom my peers enjoyed. As a result I started to limit my religious practices to only special religious days.

We also started to question the unjust distribution of wealth in our country because of Western cultural impact. Along with other students I believed the major cause of poverty in Iran was the misuse of the country's wealth and its rich oil reserves. Our fight against the regime was mainly expressed through our opinions, and they went virtually unnoticed. Whenever revolutionary-minded students got together to discuss the nation's problems we voiced our desire for our leaders to have a parental heart for their nation rather than filling their own pockets. Voicing our opinions in journalism papers cost us high marks as punishment for criticizing Iranian leaders. Of course, not one of us dared link the problems directly to the Shah, the king of Iran because it was very dangerous. We were careful not to directly blame the system itself; otherwise we would have risked danger to ourselves and our loved ones. We hoped for poor students and their families to be financially supported by the government so one day they might be able to voice their opinions or play a role in the government of the country they worked so hard for. It seemed unfair that only the rich governed Iran, supporting a system that protected their own interests.

When I finished high school in 1975 I was accepted to a college in Tehran, the capital of Iran. I had never been away from my family, and it was the longest journey I ever made. I went to stay with a family in Tehran who had once spent a holiday in our village with relatives. They told me that I could not live in Tehran with the amount of savings I had and offered me a room in their home with food three times a day for 3500 riyals[1] a month. At the time that equaled about fifty US dollars. I was taken aback by the family's request for money because such an invitation never involved a monetary exchange. It was a cultural embarrassment to even suggest payment while you yourself are enjoying free food and holiday with relatives and friends. I was desperate to move to Tehran so didn't give their demands much thought. I agreed to live with them and pay monthly rent.

I moved into their home soon after. I quickly discovered that unlike traditional Iranian culture the mother of the family was the decision maker. There were also many questionable situations that caused me to wonder about the family's moral values. They seemed quite different at home than what I saw on their vacation in Talesh. It also puzzled me that I couldn't

1   The *riyal* is the Iranian unit of currency.

44

discern what jobs the family members held. They seemed to be trying to keep the specifics of their employment secret. This might normally be the case if someone was engaged in work that was criminal in nature or less prestigious or even immoral. It was a strange eye-opener living with these people because they were so radically different than the family unit I was accustomed to. However my desire to pursue my education put off deeper thoughts about the family's bizarre behavior.

Avoiding Temptation

If this family was peculiar and difficult to figure out, I was certain about one thing—the motives of the youngest member of the family. She was in the eleventh grade and her attitude toward me was troubling. This girl was set on involving herself in my life. I had come to Tehran with the hope that I would study and graduate from the university and thoughts of girls were far from my mind. I did desire to build a relationship with a young and beautiful city girl some day but not with this girl from a family that led such a secretive life.

I sat alone studying in my room one day and this girl entered without knocking. Even letting her into my room when no one was home was dangerous in Islamic society. In Islam a young man is forbidden to communicate with a girl unless she is engaged to him. Even among nominal Muslims the communication process cannot be lengthy unless this is permitted through the involvement of senior family members. Younger girls and boys who do not follow these principles can be forced to marry each other in order to preserve the honor of their families. Therefore, any tolerance of this girl's advances would force me to marry her. I couldn't afford to allow anyone to see her alone with me in my room.

I was afraid and asked her to leave the room but she ignored me. I wanted to force her out but quickly decided against it. Instead, I left the house calmly and waited outside in the street. Soon after, one of her brothers, the friendliest of the bunch, returned. Fearfully I explained what had transpired with his sister. I was so relieved when he turned his face away and said, "I know that little evil one." We returned to his home where he approached his sister and exclaimed "If this man tells me once again that you were in his room, I will kill you!" He waited there until his parents arrived and warned them to be aware of the hardship the girl had created for me. This was a great favor he did for me.

Homesick

I missed my family so much during the first months in Tehran that I would make the eight-hour trek home every weekend. The lifestyle in Tehran was unbearable to me. In smaller cities and villages we not only cared for our family members and relatives but also for others, even strangers. In Tehran people seemed to care only for immediate family members. To make ends meet people in the city were willing to cross ethical boundaries. I wanted to run away and take refuge in my village even if only for two days each week. However the constant traveling back and forth to Talesh was quickly drying up all the money I had saved for tuition, so I learned to live independently of my family and my visits to Talesh became less frequent.

My landlord's daughter continued to cause problems. After she became sure that I had no interest in her she started to become hostile towards me in her family's absence. One day I lost my temper and said to her, "You were forbidden to come to my room. If you continue to do so, I will throw you out." She taunted me, saying, "Wait until my mum comes, and I will teach you how you can kick me out of my house." Whatever it was that she told her mother became the grounds for my dismissal. My landlord's wife was abrupt. "Take your belongings and leave the house now," she said. I said to her, "You are not serious? Where can I go, without having a place? I need time to find a place." This was not the agreement that we had made when I moved from Talesh, but without a contract I had no grounds for a formal dispute.

Homeless

I took all my belongings and left the house in the early afternoon. It was the end of the month, and I had only 180 riyals left in my pocket and nowhere to go. I couldn't even afford a taxi. In shock, I wandered the streets until I remembered one of my older brother's friends rented a room in one of the poor areas of the city. I had visited him in the early days of my arrival in Tehran to pass on my brother's greetings. He and his wife rented a single room on the ground floor of the apartment and were living in it with their four children. There was a shared toilet outside the room under the steps to the second floor that was used by first-floor residents. The only shower was at a public bath.

I knew this poor friend did not have enough room for me but I believed he would help me in my time of need. I dared to ask a taxi driver for a lift, explaining my plight and offering all I had. The driver agreed to my offer and drove me to my friend's apartment.

I knocked, but no one opened the door. I knocked again. A neighbor came out and told me that my friend no longer lived there. The news was heavy on my heart. The man asked me, "Did he invite you here without letting you know what happened to him?" I explained my situation, telling him of my need. As we talked the landlord approached and said he remembered me from my visit. With this little bit of credibility I felt confident to ask if I could store my belongings there. The landlord said, "I know your friend. He is a good man. I have a great respect for him. For his sake, I can help you and keep your belongings in my store room." His generosity lightened my burden. I left my bags in his storeroom, thanked him, and headed for school—a two-and-a-half-hour walk.

Under a Bridge

"O my God," I thought. "Where am I going to sleep tonight? What is going to happen to me? What I am going to eat?" I cried out to God. With no money and three days left until the end of month, when I received a monthly student allowance, I had no solution to my situation. It threatened every aspect of my life, including my university education, in which I had invested my heart and mind from a very young age.

I had always desired to become an educated man, for as long as I remember. I knew that a life of disadvantage could prevent me from going to college. Knowing this drove me to work hard at my studies and to save money. I was also eager to win the favor of my father. I wanted to assure him that because of my education I would never be a burden to him financially. It was my dream to graduate, find a job and help my family overcome poverty. Everybody in my hometown knew that I was a hard worker and zealous to become an educated man. It was well-known that I was working hard to pursue my future dreams and I was willing to endure a good measure of hardship to achieve my goals. Some parents thought of me as a role model for their children, even though many of them were still amazed that I was accepted into the university.

Now I would be denied the opportunity to complete what I had started because of the situation that had befallen me with the lies of my landlord's daughter. The failure to complete my education would make me lose face and dishonor my family in Talesh. My mind was racing with so many different thoughts and questions and I didn't know what to do. Should I call my family and let them know, so they could sell everything they had and send the money to me? How could I tell any of this to my father who never showed any interest in my education apart from what might bring him personal gain? He would make life hell for my mother and any of my family members who had encouraged my pursuit of an education.

I believed that an education could open up political and social doors for me in Iranian society. I could acquire respectability that country boys seldom enjoy. This sudden setback would be a major defeat for my political goals. My poverty would hinder my progress. As a student in Talesh it was always my desire to see the success of all less privileged students in the country. I had many friends who were not able to study and only one of my eleven siblings was able to complete school through the ninth grade. It was heartbreaking to me that the country was led only by wealthy autocrats. And it wasn't merely that the country was run by the rich but their attitudes towards rural citizens was one bent on degradation and humiliation. These political and social pressures enslaved my people. I labored under the belief that education was the key to demolishing such injustices, and it could lead the less privileged classes to political positions that would allow them to have a voice in their own country. Education was the great equalizer, or so I thought.

As I tried to sort out all the thoughts running through my head I made my way to a bridge in Tehran called "The Bridge of Hafez". I felt very tired and needed to sit for a few moments and the only quiet place I could find was under the bridge. I found a spot under one of the beams, sat on an old newspaper, leaned on the beam and tried to rest. The decisions I faced were not easy to think about and I was unsure of how I could build the courage to act. I was filled with shame and so afraid that someone would see me sitting under the bridge like the homeless man I was. After a while I began to feel hungry. I tried to ignore my stomach but the pangs wouldn't let me rest. Suddenly, I remembered that I had a piece of bread in my pocket. Before the landlord's wife kicked me out of the house I knew that I had 180 riyals and I would be able to survive on that until I received my monthly student stipend. But in that moment when I was frantically gathering my belongings to leave, I realized that my problem was bigger than the 180 riyals in my pocket. I retrieved a piece of bread that I had discarded in the small rubbish bin in my room. I couldn't have known that the bread that had meant so little to me that morning would become both my lunch and my dinner on the very same day. And if I didn't find a way out of my situation quickly, it might also be the last piece of bread I would eat for a very long time.

The bitterness of homelessness and my hunger were wounding my heart so deeply. I started to complain to God: "Where are you, God? For years I have spoken to you. I always thought you were the only one who would help me. How many times do I have to call on you? Should I call to you again? Who else is going to help me if you are the sovereign God?" The hopelessness in my heart was overwhelming. "O Tehran!" I said "You do not know what friendship is." A favorite saying in Iran is "Who is who in Tehran? The dogs do not know their masters."

The pain of loss and uncertainty was heavy, so I bowed my head to rest. I tried to lie down but the concrete was not smooth. I stood and saw a corner under the bridge where some boxes were spread. I walked over and could see that someone had already slept there. I was too tired to think anymore so I laid myself down and slept. I couldn't tell how long I had slept because I didn't have a watch. It was ironic to consider that I could not even make a home there on the cardboard box where I had slept, because it was already someone else's home. I looked around and there was plenty of space but deep inside I was concerned for my safety. It never occurred to me, even as I stood there a homeless man, that not all homeless people are drunks and addicts.

Caring Friends

Another concern began to plague my thoughts: Where would I shower, wash my clothes, shave or brush my teeth? Tears filled my eyes. The fear of my unforeseeable future consumed me. Lost in my despair, I headed toward the university. I went to a campus café and sat in a corner. One of my classmates saw me and sat down. We were not close friends but we had spoken a few times. He knew about the problems I had with my landlord's daughter and he had also shared some of his problems with me.

My classmate asked, "Is anything wrong? You look worried." He could see the pain and uncertainty in my face. I hesitated to share my predicament with him, ashamed of my poverty. Culturally, one only confides in family members; strangers might listen but not out of any genuine concern or willingness to help. Recognizing my apprehension to open up, my fellow student said, "I know that I haven't been able to establish a strong friendship with you, but could you please accept me as your brother and let me know your burden? I promise to help you as a friend." His genuine compassion touched my heart, and I told him of the circumstances that I found myself in. "Tonight I am going to sleep under the Bridge of Hafez," I told him. My new "brother" looked at me with shock and his eyes welled up with tears. He quickly excused himself to use the phone.

My friend called four other classmates and arranged for us to meet with them under the Bridge of Hafez without telling me. When he told me I was embarrassed that he had told others, but he enlightened me as to the deeper meaning of the situation. "We have to be embarrassed," he said. "The rulers of this country must be embarrassed that a fellow citizen, the future generation of this country, is sleeping under a bridge. Let our friends come and see how it is to sleep under the bridge."

I left the café with my friend to meet our classmates under the Bridge of Hafez. There were other street kids there who had already made their beds for the night. Our friends asked why they were called to this place, and my friend said, "Our classmate will sleep here tonight because his landlord kicked him out. I wanted you to see how it would be if the same thing happened to one of us. We need to help our friend by finding a solution to his problem." One of them said, "My landlord has gone for a week-long trip to his hometown. I can take him to my room after dark. We need to keep it a secret for a few days as we search for a room for him to rent."

Rental prospects for poor and middle class students were very slim because the government did not want students gathering to plot against the ruling system. This caused landlords to become cautious about renting to students. If any rentals did become available, they came with very rigid conditions.

My friend however made it clear to other classmates that my student money would not be in for a few days. They all chipped in enough for me to get by. I accepted their amazingly generous offer and within a few days I found a small storeroom in someone's yard to rent for 3500 riyals a month. The ceiling of this store room was so low that I was not able to stand straight up without hitting my head.

I had very little money left for food after paying my monthly rent. Sometimes friends brought bread to me but there were times when I had no choice but to rummage through garbage cans to find something to eat. My friends who knew about my situation found a landlord who was willing to rent a two-bedroom apartment to four of us for 16,000 riyals. They allowed me to pay only 2,500 riyals and divided the remaining portion of 1500 riyals among them. To show my gratitude I decided to work hard to complete my education ahead of the four-year schedule, so I completed my Bachelor's degree in three years.

Angry with God

The hardships I faced in Tehran caused me to be angry with God. In Islam Allah is the creator of every calamity and the source all pains.[2] Even though I believed this, I expected to see hardships in other people's lives but certainly not in my own. I believed that because I had tried my best and prayed diligently and lived a good life that he would show me favor. My obvious expectations of Allah were that, because of the obedience with

---

2   Q57:22. (This abbreviation means Qur'an, Sura 57 verse 22.)

which I had served him, he would help me. I was more than dismayed when I found myself deserted.

It was 1975 when the political regime lost its full control over universities. Students were finally able to meet secretly to discuss problems or their beliefs. I heard some of my classmates rejecting the existence of God, since He was invisible, inaccessible and unhelpful. I already had a good excuse to share their views with them. So I ignored Allah and became involved with atheist and communist groups. I even called myself atheist after a while. I really didn't understand atheism or communism but my anger toward Allah provoked me to engage myself in godless activities. I gradually began to doubt God's existence. "Who is God?" I asked myself. "If I don't see him or his help and cannot touch him, this means he does not exist." Universities were quickly becoming hotbeds of secret discussions about beliefs and ideas beyond Islam and I began to lean toward students who were espousing communism.

I read books about communism that were distributed secretly among the students. It was still dangerous for students to openly gather to discuss religion or any ideology that might pose a threat to the regime in Iran. Revolutionary students would gather in the mountains, in the northern part of Tehran. Students could escape during weekends, as so many people often went to the mountains for picnics. They used this as a cover but their time was spent planning Iran's future. Two major groups developed who claimed to be against the regime. They were the Communists and the Fundamentalist Muslims, each with their own subgroups. At the weekend "retreats," thousands of students went mountain climbing and sang revolutionary songs. The Shah's civil police were there to spy on the students and they caught, tortured, and even killed some of them. Nevertheless, the mountains were still more secure for the students than the city.

Some of my classmates were involved with the Fundamentalist Islamic groups. I had the opportunity to discuss creation and evolution with them. Interesting doctrinal and philosophical questions were raised, some of which were hard to understand. I studied books about both doctrines in order to take a clear stand. Through my studies I realized that the world could not have been created by itself; I knew that there must be a divine Creator for the universe. This realization eventually led me to join the Fundamentalist Islamic students and help to overthrow the kingdom of Iran and bring the Ayatollah Khomeini into power. We blamed the Shah for the widespread poverty in a country that had such rich oil resources.

4

The Ayatollah Khomeini

A New Leader for Iran

I had problems with the socio-political system in Iran like many other students. Why should a student struggle with poverty and be forced to sleep on the street in a rich, oil based country and be threatened with the termination of his studies when he is working tirelessly for his future. These conditions made me angry towards the Shah. The country was rich but only for rich people who had built stronger relationship with high rank governmental officers. Middle class citizens, villagers and students suffered. It wasn't hard to find motives to join the students' revolutionary movement against the Iranian government.

Gradually I became zealous in my opposition of the Shah's regime but I still did not have a clear ideological path in Islam. My belief in the existence of a divine Creator did not mean that I really understood all aspects of Islam's philosophy. I had joined the Islamic group only because they believed the world was created by God and also were questioning the economic injustice in Iran. We did not have the resources to study other religions and did not have time to indulge in a deeper study of Islam and its political, economic, social, and ethical principles, to decide if Islam would give us a better future. We did not understand how our society would change under the rule of Islam. We were told that Islam was the solution for everything and if we expected to be the best nation in the world we must follow the mullahs and commit ourselves to the Ayatollah Khomeini who was sent into exile in 1963 by the Shah and living in Iraq. The mullahs also told us that discussion about the future was not a priority since the Shah, the cause of all injustice, was in power. The first and most urgent step for overcoming injustice was to get rid of the Shah. The mullahs were able to progressively establish a strong connection between us and the Ayatollah Khomeini and prepare us to follow his instructions diligently.

Saddam Hussein, the president of Iraq, eventually forced the Ayatollah Khomeini to leave Iraq. In October 1978 he made his way to France. While in France he continued to organize his return to Iran from the new foreign headquarters. The Ayatollah was a convincing speaker and seemingly a stronger leader than the Shah. His opposition to the Shah was favored by some contemporary Western leaders who wanted Islamic theocracy as a shield against the influence of Russian Communism. The Ayatollah wisely tailored his messages to be less religious and more economic and socio-political in order to encourage resistance to the Shah's regime. He wanted support from non-religious and nominal Muslims as well. But under the surface, the Ayatollah's opposition was neither political nor social nor economic. It was in reality a result of the Shah's acceptance of Israel as a Jewish country which violated Islamic obligations. Jews, according to Islam, do not deserve to have anything or any land. The Shah was an apostate in the eyes of the Ayatollah and had to be removed from leadership and killed.

Despite Islam's intolerance of atheism, the Ayatollah Khomeini even invited atheists to join the revolutionary movement. He never spoke publicly against any non-Muslim groups that were against the Shah before the Revolution. His overriding goal was to gain power among the public in order to overthrow the kingdom of the Shah, and for this reason he needed the unity of all groups, if only temporarily.

Despite Khomeini's hypocrisy to various opposition groups his tactics worked among the masses. They were frustrated at the repressive economic and political system in place and unable to discern Khomeini's true underlying motives. He was able to persuade revolutionaries that his intention was to rescue Iran from economic hardship and dictatorship set up by the ruling government. He made Iranians believe he would establish equal opportunity among all groups in Iran. He continually announced that freedom and democracy were the rights of every Iranian but the Shah had stolen them. Economic prosperity was certain for Iran because of its oil but the Shah abused its wealth and left many citizens with little. The Ayatollah based his propaganda on these issues to win Iranian support. We believed his claims because of the hardships Iranians faced under the Shah's rule. Never did we imagine that when he attained power he would disregard Iranian well-being and sacrifice human rights; all to establish authoritarian Islamic government and terrorism.

The mullahs also who were the close companions to the Ayatollah Khomeini never spoke against atheism or other religious groups but against the current injustices in Iran. They encouraged us to be more zealous in fighting the Shah. We thought that they were encouraging us to help demolish injustice and establish justice. We never thought they did not care about justice at all and only wanted to establish Islamic rule that would subject its people to Islamic law, the Shari'a. We based our obedience and allegiance blindly on their propaganda that Islam was the most superior religion and could lead the country to democracy. We never studied Islam closely enough to see how genuine the Ayatollah and other mullahs were in their claims.

Like many others I believed that Islam could address the inconsistencies of our culture, close the gap between rich and poor, and lead us to democracy. We did not realize the heart of Islam was incompatible with freedom and democracy. The Ayatollah Khomeini's proclamation of freedom delivered a landslide victory for him and his committed mullahs, so that they gained wealth and power but it blocked the country's path to freedom. By our surrender to the Ayatollah Khomeini we became our own worst enemies, handing over our country to the mullahs who made our motherland a prison.

Revolutionary

The Revolution caused me to strongly attach myself to political Islam and stay close to Muslim Fundamentalists. I found a place in my heart for Muslims involved in terrorism against the Shah's officials and those who had fought Israelis in Palestine, Lebanon and other Islamic countries. The Shah killed some of these Muslims while imprisoning or exiling others. Those in exile or prison sent messages to encourage us to resist the Shah before the Revolution. We secretly distributed their messages, books, essays and audio cassettes to people to unify resistance to the Shah. This revolutionary idea occupied our hearts and minds so we tried every means to weaken the Shah's rule.

The Shah's regime tried every possible way to suffocate the revolutionary movement. One day, before dawn, civil police invaded our apartment looking for any evidence of our involvement with terrorist Muslims. Thanks to one of our neighbors we were warned in advance and before the police raided we removed all the revolutionary literature we had collected.

In less than two years revolutionary books were distributed everywhere and openly sold in streets. The Shah's government was not able to remove the books anymore and could not control the situation.

Our activities to fuel the Revolution drew the attention of many young people. Believing somehow that they could empower the revolutionaries, they burned banks, public houses and buses in nationwide protest.

Daniel as a revolutionary student in 1977

Hometown Revolutionary

After completing college in 1978 I returned to my hometown, Talesh, in Gilan, the northern state of Iran. Gilan was pro-Shah and closed off to the spread of the revolutionary mind-set. Why? Gilan's musical culture was not compatible with the fundamentalist Islam of the Ayatollah Khomeini which was anti-music, its seashore attracted non-religious tourists who spread a western way of life, and the Shah himself, who favored western culture, came from the north. My hometown had a fourth reason. Many people were bound by a feudal and tribal heritage and their words carried weight among the native Taleshis. Many locals walked miles from the villages to the city to express their support for the Shah. The Shah had lost support in many states but the people of Northern Iran were working hard and hoping to give him moral support to maintain power. The opposition in other states were outspoken but not in Talesh. So I worked hard along with other revolutionary men and women to spread the spirit of the Revolution in the area.

My activities allowed me to advance as an Islamic leader even though I was still unaware of the true nature of Islam. I knew only the superficial rites and rituals, enough to be a Muslim. I knew how to wash, how and when to stand for prayer, what to not handle, taste, or touch. This was the extent of the Islamic knowledge of most radical Muslims. We were taught to imitate and follow Muhammad, his successors and religious leaders. We were gradually indoctrinated to believe that there must be no choice when it comes to Islam. If Muhammad, as the superman of Islam, was forced by the angel to follow Allah, what choice did we have except to follow Islam?[1]

Our commitment to the Ayatollah Khomeini grew day after day. Soon I began to look like him and act like him. I even desired to become a mullah like him, and dressed in a cleric's cloak[2]. We believed Khomeini to be the best contemporary follower of Muhammad, and we tried our best to fulfill his orders and instructions, inciting riots against the Shah to force him to leave the country.

By 1978 bookshops were overflowing with propaganda that fueled the Revolution. The Shah was losing power and it seemed as though everyone's thoughts in urban areas were focused on overthrowing him.

---

1   Muhammad said that he himself did not want to follow Allah, but Allah's angel became angry and was about to kill him for his rebellion, and in order to stay alive, Muhammad had no choice but to follow Allah (Ibn Hisham, *Sirat Rasul Allah*, and p.106-107).
2   If you study in an Islamic college and graduate, you wear the mullah's uniform, the *abaa* (cloak) and *amaameh* (headband).

I joined the army to serve the mandatory two-year military obligation in the meantime and was sent to the Garrison of Esfahan, located in the middle of Iran, south of Tehran. The Garrison of Esfahan trains in ground-to-air fighting techniques using various tanks. I was trained on the 23mm tank. A substantial number of other students there were also revolutionaries and we began to hold secret meetings to plan a unified effort of religious and non-religious soldiers to destroy the hierarchy of the Garrison. We encouraged all students and soldiers to violate the regulations and policies of their commanders, and caused chaos in the mess hall and during different programs whenever the general commander was present. Unable to discipline everyone the Garrison authorities quickly lost control.

The commanders sought the major revolutionary leaders, who had incited the insubordination, to kill them. I managed to escape to Tehran where it was easy to hide and work with other revolutionaries. We did whatever we could to bring the Shah down from his throne and we opened the way for the Ayatollah Khomeini to come back to Iran. We held streets protests, broke and burned government buildings and vehicles. By this time the Shah lost western support, especially the support of his best ally, America. He and his family left Iran and selected a prime minister to temporarily rule the country until his return.

A King Dethroned

The Air Force joined the revolutionaries when the Shah left on January 16, 1979, rendering the government incapable of controlling public demonstrations and riots. The army continued to lose power. I did not need to hide anymore so I went back to my hometown to be with my family and to stir the people of that area against the Shah's ruling prime minister.

The majority of the people in my hometown fought against the revolutionary movement with propaganda favoring the Shah's kingdom. The political mind-set of the area was more of a feudalist autocratic one serving the causes of upper-class citizens who did not want the lower-class mullahs and others to have a place in the political hierarchy. It was easy to maintain favor for the Shah. The people believed heads of communities, or the aristocracy, were able to better relate to parliamentarians, senators or politicians and revive the kingdom that had run for thousands of years in Iran. This autocratic leadership was interwoven into the people's way of life and the natives felt obligated to bow down in front of the autocrats. When these feudal lords called the people to resist the revolutionaries the people obeyed and pledged their allegiance to this call. Only the younger educated generations, who were still a minority, favored change and adventure and were receptive to fighting against the system.

Some of the area's mullahs were fiscally obligated to local leaders and showed no interest in the Revolution. After their speeches in mosques, they always prayed "long live the Shah and his kingdom". However, after the Revolution, they all claimed to be revolutionaries. The key revolutionary mullahs in the capital city of Tehran diverted the socio-political path of the Revolution into a strictly religious undertaking and employed a majority of the mullahs who had previously served autocrats, the kingdom or remained neutral. According to Khomeini's law those mullahs who were in the service of the Shah's regime had to be sentenced to imprisonment or death. They supported a king who maintained friendly relations with Israel and was pro-West. Khomeini spared them however because they were clerics and clerics had to have more rights than others according to Islam.

As Khomeini became a shelter for these mullahs after the Revolution, they also became shelters for many of their past autocratic masters—in exchange for monetary payoffs. The former oppressors found protection from the threats of young revolutionaries who wanted to hold them accountable for their injustices. Some of the former autocratic leaders were even given military and governmental positions and made life miserable for those who were once the arms and legs of the Revolution. They now held positions that allowed them to torture and kill those revolutionaries who were fighting for democracy. I was once beaten by a few of these ex-autocrats a year after the Revolution, falling unconscious in the street.

The Ayatollah Khomeini quickly entered the scene after the Shah vacated his thrown and Iran. It was a momentous occasion for me and all who had fought against the Shah's rule. Khomeini's arrival on February 1st, 1979 also signaled defeat for the army who eventually surrendered. The Shah's government collapsed, his appointed prime minister escaped, and the revolutionaries took over. Tears of happiness flowed freely from all who supported the Revolution, making Khomeini's return to Iran a day of celebration. We had overthrown the most powerful government in the Middle-East and believed that we had opened the door for all Iranians to take part in governing of their country and advancing prosperity. What a heartbreak only months after the Revolution when we learned our zealous allegiance to the Ayatollah Khomeini and his surrounding mullahs had been abused and our plans for Iran's future had been ignored for the sake of establishing the theocratic rule of Islam.

PREPARED
TO
SERVE

5

Life after the Revolution

A Political Religion

The Ayatollah Khomeini ordered those who deserted the army in the name of the Revolution to return to their military positions. He wanted to strengthen the country's fighting forces. I also returned to my army post to answer to his command. I discovered that I was the only person who ran away from the garrison during the Revolution. This seemed to gain me a great measure of fame and respect among my co-workers.

The Revolution had caused a break in the chain of command so that the military suffered difficulties imposing disciplinary action and implementing normal decision making. Officially we were expected to obey the orders of our superior officers and commanders, but now we received orders informally from the local mullah whose authority trumped that of the officers. The revolutionary mindset was to dismiss top army officials or condemn them because of their loyalty to the Shah. The mullahs believed

Daniel after returning back to the army at the end of 1979

the structure and values of the army were not an acceptable reflection of Islam and everything was now expected to align itself with the religion.

I did little but preach Islam while in the army. I also learned that our colonel, Sayyad Shirazi, was a very religious Muslim man but had managed to keep his religious life a secret before the Revolution. It was dangerous for army officers to practice their religion openly while under the Shah's rule. Colonel Shirazi had been able to establish a strong relationship with an influential local religious leader, the Ayatollah Taheri. After the Revolution he connected to us revolutionaries and then became the middle man between us and Ayatollah Taheri. Ayatollah Taheri led the religious men of the garrison, including myself, to meet Ayatollah Khomeini in Qom. Qom is the religious shrine where the Ayatollah Khomeini trained and first announced his opposition to Shah in 1963 for the Shah's tolerance and friendliness towards America and Israel. The Ayatollah Khomeini chose Qom as his residence after the Revolution because he promised Iranians that he and the mullahs would not get involved in politics but only attend to religious affairs. Khomeini's close companions such as the Ayatollahs Rafsanjani and Khamenei (his successor) and a few others caused him to change his mind, and he later moved to Tehran.

When we met Khomeini we assured him of our zeal to convert Iran into a radical Islamic country and that we were also ready to build the army of Allah (*Hezbollah*[1]) to establish the rule of Islam in Iran and abroad. Some of us however did not know the real meaning of Islamic rule practically. The Ayatollah Taheri was our spokesman and through him we tried to convince the Ayatollah Khomeini that we were skilled military men ready

---

1   The word *Hezbollah* was used commonly for the first time in Iran after the 1979 Revolution. The followers of Ayatollah Khomeini were called Hezbollah. With the encouragement and support of ruling mullahs in Iran, the Shiite militias in Lebanon adopted this name for themselves.

to teach Iranians fighting techniques, and terrorist and suicide tactics in order to send them to conquer and destroy all infidels, including Israel and the United States.

The Ayatollah Taheri was the most powerful mullah in Isfahan at that time, gaining his religious popularity in the typical manner.[2] He was also one of the most influential religious leaders in Iran because he had amassed so many

Daniel visited the Ayatollah Khomeini in the city of Qom towards the end of 1979

followers. Every clergy who becomes an Ayatollah has authority to accumulate his own followers (imitators). His popularity meant that he had a say about everything in Iran and his opposition could be very costly to both secular and religious leaders, especially to those who wanted to ignore his power.

The Shah of Iran lost his power and the support of his people to Muslim clerics because of their great influence over the

---

2 A student of Islam must reach a special religious level to obtain the position of *Ayatollah*, which means a sign of Allah or a sign of godliness. After finishing religious studies, Islamic students are sent by the head of their school to a town or city in order to preach and teach in a mosque. These religious clergymen and leaders establish themselves in Islamic societies through many years of living in the community, and every clergy who becomes an Ayatollah has the authority to gather his own followers.

people throughout the kingdom of Shah. The Shah aimed to lead people to adopt a western life-style but he did not know how to deal with Islam which was against western democracy. The mullahs took advantage of people's ignorance and stirred them against the Shah. Shortly after the Revolution however, the ruling Islamic Government also lost much of its influence and popularity with Iranian citizens. Some of the more prominent Ayatollahs of the country were being ignored by the new ruling authorities. These Ayatollahs who had many followers criticized the government in the Islamic Republic of Iran. The Ayatollahs even went so far as to condemn the new regime's activities as anti-Islamic.

However, the Ayatollah Taheri led us to Qom with the underlying motive to spread the subtle news that Islam was a political religion and it is mullahs, more than secular people, who ought to be active in politics and the Islamization of Iran and the world. This contradicted the early promise of the Ayatollah Khomeini who had promised the separation of church and state in government. The Ayatollah Taheri and other influential mullahs knew that the Ayatollah Khomeini had used the Islamic doctrine of *taqiyya* (pious deception) to hide his plan for theocracy since the start of the Revolution. He did this to incite people against the Shah in order to attain power. Now, he was in power and needed the mullahs, like Taheri, to prepare the mind of the majority secular-minded people for the mullahs' take-over.

The Shah had fled the country by this time and Khomeini's partisanship against the Shah was no longer enough to yoke us to Khomeini. He had to use different deceptive tactics, not only to protect himself from the consequences of his lies, but also to establish a law to punish those of us who did not want to tolerate them.

The mullahs started to raise their voices, saying that without the political leadership of the Ayatollah Khomeini the country might descend into chaos. Subtly and progressively they convinced many Iranians that not only did the Ayatollah Khomeini deserve to be the supreme political leader in Iran but also the sovereign leader (Velayat'e Faghih) who would have absolute right over every citizen and indeed everything in Iran.

While the radical mullahs were busy establishing themselves in Iran, another prominent clergyman, the Ayatollah Hassan Lahouti was working to establish a revolutionary army. Iran already had a powerful army but Muslim leaders did not trust the commanders of an army who had once sworn their allegiance to the Shah. Also, a majority of army officers were trained as patriots in order to love their country and protect it against its enemies. Such patriotism is rejected in Islam. If a country is not ruled by Islam, both national pious Muslims and foreign pious Muslims have the right to attack secular Muslim patriots and capture the country. That is why so many committed Muslims in the world are in one way or the other linked to Palestinian leaders and Hezbollah: these radical Muslims groups were able to Islamize their people rapidly, destroy nominalism in their lands, and achieve great success in fighting against Israel.

So for the Ayatollahs, the Muslim militias had to hold more power than the general army officers. Khomeini was also bent on taking over power in other countries and this could only be accomplished through the establishment of a radically zealous band of fanatical Muslims: Hezbollah. As a result, the Ayatollah Lahouti called on the Ayatollah Taheri to help him seek out skilled soldiers who also happened to be religious zealots. The Ayatollah Taheri contacted Colonel Shirazi and asked him to take part in their plan to build this new army and to encourage like-minded Muslims to join up.

Finding Favor

Because of our religious zeal, I and another garrison companion had earned a good reputation and were invited by Colonel Shirazi to accompany him to Tehran to establish the new revolutionary army with the Ayatollah Lahouti. We prepared ourselves to depart from Isfahan to Tehran. We were delayed in leaving when the Ayatollah Taheri said we had to wait because there was tension between the mullahs surrounding the Ayatollah Khomeini and the Ayatollah Lahouti over the establishment of a revolutionary army. The mullahs such as Rafsanjani, Beheshti, and Khamenei (the present grand Ayatollah and successor of the Ayatollah Khomeini) did not want the Ayatollah Lahouti to be in charge of establishing the revolutionary army because they did not view him as sufficiently radical enough and in line with them. Revolutionaries are required to be emotionally indifferent, insensitive, and zealous to impose Islam on others at all costs. It seemed that the Ayatollah Lahouti did not possess enough of a terrorist mind-set nor did he seem willing to ignore the right of his fellow citizens in the name of the Islamic cause.

Internal Chaos

The Ayatollah Lahouti showed tolerance towards the existence of all other parties, even atheists, because he believed that unity among the existing groups would strengthen the country's stand against Israel and the Christian world.

In contrast, the mullahs' disunity would not only hinder the spread of the Revolution but would also disarm its goals. The Ayatollah Lahouti's logic directly opposed Islam in that Islam seeks to triumph and eradicate all other beliefs[3]. His problem was that he was more nationalistic than the Ayatollah Khomeini, who preferred the nomadic and hostile culture of Saudi Arabia. The Ayatollah Lahouti was also not in favor of killing his fellow citizens because of infidelity. His values sharply contrasted the commands of Muhammad, the prophet of Islam, who killed all his opponents in Saudi Arabia and only freed those who submitted to Islam and its army. The above mentioned mullahs who opposed the Ayatollah Lahouti

---

3   Q9:33; 48:28.

wanted to disarm him and remove him from any position or power but he refused to step down. Soon after he was mysteriously murdered.

The injustices perpetrated by our revered leaders created tensions in Iran and disappointed and confused those of us who had contributed a lot towards the victory of the Revolution and now were waiting to reap the fruits of our work. Alas, we

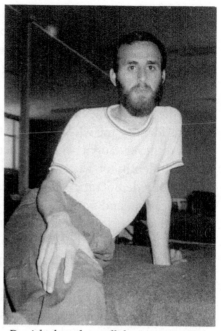

Daniel when the mullahs were struggling for power at the beginning of 1980

were much younger, less experienced and unaware of the bitterness of Islamic politics. We did not have a proficient knowledge of Islamic history. We had history courses, but these covered only a limited selection of subjects. We had not been taught that Arab Amirs (caliphs), and Safavid, Afshar and Ghajar dynasties, who ruled over Iran, had degraded Iranian culture and persecuted their opponents and non-Muslims for the sake of radical Islam. We were raised to be largely illiterate concerning the political philosophies of the various Muslim groups in our history. Because of this we were not able to discern the root of our country's problems, which was Islam. The Shah's fear of radical Muslim leaders spread political correctness, and thereby we lost a conceptual study of history in order to arm ourselves with the wisdom sufficient to understand politics. The Shah knew with Islam he would not be able to associate himself with the great kings of old, Cyrus and Darius. Instead, he put himself forward as a faithful Muslim to overcome the opposition of committed Muslims.

He was not living according to the standards of Islam, but emphatically called himself a devoted Muslim. Because of his superficial proclamation, we were also calling ourselves Muslims proudly, without knowing that Islamists hated our nation's democratic values.

From the early grades we were taught about the roots of our cultural identity and why we needed to be proud of it. However we were never taught who had been posing threats to our national identity or what we needed to reject or embrace to protect our democratic values. These problems ran deep in our education, and not only negatively affected us in making reasoned choices for our country's future, but kept us ignorant until we lost our country to its sworn enemies, the mullahs. The real enemy was hidden under political correctness. The strong values we adhered to, which kept the nation together, were vulnerable to the threats of Islam and eventually were belittled and dominated by Islamists.

We felt confusion by the conflict between what we had perceived to be messages of democracy, peace and hope for Iran and what we were seeing now after the Revolution. Not only were the revolutionary mullahs eager to slaughter non-Muslims, but even their own devoted Muslim colleagues who opposed them. The swift political rise of the mullahs, which deprived their opponents of opportunities to react, incited hostile rejection. We were perplexed to observe that even seemingly small matters could cause bloodshed between Muslims leaders.

The contention among Muslim religious leaders spread quickly to other religious and non-religious groups and even to our military forces, causing widespread chaos. This chaotic atmosphere worked to the advantage of the mullahs, who knew that if they were to be successful in imposing Islam throughout Iran, they would have to create chaos first and then disarm their opponents quickly no matter the cost.

As a result we were dismissed and exempted from fulfilling the remaining part of our two years commitment to the Iranian Army. From Isfahan I went to Tehran to find a suitable place to live, and serve the Revolution and my country if possible.

The Ayatollah Khomeini had appointed Mr Bazargan as interim prime minister due to his popularity among the revolutionaries. However, he was not permitted to establish his cabinet members independently. Khomeini's close associates among the clergy put pressure on him and took part in his government despite their dislike of Bazargan's philosophy of running the country. Bazargan was a committed Muslim and the leader of the Liberation Movement [Party] but the mullahs did not favor his nationalistic approach to governing the country. Even though they had junior roles in Bazargan's government, they gained more power than him due to their close relationship with Khomeini. They knew that it would not be easy for them to have major governmental roles over freedom-loving people. They took less important roles in order to change the atmosphere first, paving the ground for dominance in the future. They were clever enough to use Bazargan's milder philosophy as a channel for penetration and destruction so that in time they could establish their own theocratic government, based on Sharia, the rigid Islamic principles. The seed of authoritarianism was sown during the time of Bazargan, and the battle for control won during the time of Dr Bani Sadr, the first Islamic president after the Revolution.

Both Bazargan and Bani Sadr knew how the mullahs betrayed the democracy pioneers in 1953, twenty six years before the Revolution of 1979, when the Prime Minister of that time, Dr Mohammad Mosaddegh, stood against the foreign policy of the Shah concerning oil, and forced him to leave the country. Bazargan himself was a part of democratic movement and also a member of Dr Mossaddegh's cabinet. He experienced the mullahs' betrayals personally in the way they first supported Dr Mossaddegh, but later withdrew, so he lost to the Shah. It was sad that he and Bani Sadr forgot or wanted to forget what the mullahs did to our country and in this way misguided us. We also believed that the mullahs would never again deceive their nation, but they did. They used new acts of deception to gain power progressively. They hid their intention to creating a despotic government behind the false promises of Khomeini to establish democracy.

While speaking pro-democratic language, the mullahs subtly encouraged their followers (not more than two per cent) to challenge authorities in every organization in order to weaken Bazargan's Government and create anarchy to pave the way for taking power. The students they controlled challenged their professors in the universities and caused the universities to close. The employees they controlled challenged the business managers and many businesses closed down. Their ordinary followers also interfered with the lives of rank-and-file people who were not committed Muslims or non-Muslims. They pressed on until they established the Religious Police to make sure Islam permeated society at all levels, and the principles of Islam (Sharia) were in practice everywhere. With the establishment of the Religious Police and the Revolutionary Army, the highly equipped and respected army was relegated to second rank status after the Revolutionary Army.

Threats to lovers of democracy started to rise after this. They were humiliated and beaten in the streets and no one was able to protect them. The mullahs were paving the ground to create more anarchy for the soon-to-be-held election. They hoped to make it easy to get their representatives into the newly established Islamic Parliament.

Bazargan's goal was to establish an Islamic version of democracy in Iran, believing that Islam favored democracy. Like so many of us, Barzagan also did not understand that with Islam it is impossible to establish a democracy. We were zealous Muslims but we did not understand Islam fully andwere unaware of its incompatibility with democracy. We always had limited access to Islamic sources, being shielded from gaining insight into our religion. The mind-set was to blindly cling to the mullahs' advice about every matter in Islam. Non-clerics had no right to adhere to any opinion based on their own personal understandings, as this could promote apostasy. We therefore blindly followed the Ayatollah Khomeini.

Like many others, I knew on the one hand that in a democratic environment people would have the freedom to challenge, question, reject or accept willingly. We learned from our studies in universities, and from common sense, that a perfect model of democracy does not use force. It is perfect because of its superior and practical values. All other models or beliefs will perish if that which is perfect is at work.

On the other hand, I also was taught to believe Islam was the last and perfect religion come to finish the incomplete works of other prophets before Muhammad. We expected that Islam's perfection would manifest itself in peacefulness and that other religions would simply cease to exist because of Islam's "irresistible" attraction. We were taught that people in ancient Saudi Arabia rejected Islam since they did not know how to deal with perfect Islam. Allah had required an absolute allegiance to Muhammad without question since he was the prophet of the perfect Islam. They believed one had no place questioning the perfect. To challenge Islam or Muhammad carried a death sentence.[4]

The Ayatollah Khomeini's promise of freedom caused me, like many others, to believe that he would not force us to follow the ancient authoritarianism of Muhammad. Muhammad forced others to follow him because his contemporaries were ignorant (*jahil* in Arabic) and uneducated. We were educated and lived in an educated and civilized era and we were able to listen, evaluate and choose the best. The mullahs persuaded us of this before the 1979 Revolution. The narrative changed however when the Ayatollah gained power after the Revolution. Ayatollah Khomeini passed laws for any one

---

4   Q8:10-13; 33:36.

who rejected him, the one who was ruling in Muhammad's place, to be subjected to the same punishment which was applied in Muhammad's time. We all were transported back to Muhammad's ancient authoritarianism of the 7th century, and treated like the ancient ignorant ones.

Betrayed

The fanatical-minded mullahs expected all young Iranian revolutionaries to immediately assimilate to Muhammad's 1400 year old Bedouin culture, which promulgated the belief that all other groups had to disappear. They believed that their party was the only Islamic party to have the right to exist. Only the party of Allah (*Hezbollah*[5]) will triumph—so the Quran says—and we were expected to motivate our own countrymen to fulfill the commands of Muhammad against our own people.

We were unable to connect what we believed about Islam with the reality we saw unfolding around us, so we began to blame the mullahs for the violence and dissension. Without ever knowing true Islam, we called it perfect and blamed the mullahs when things began to sour. We proclaimed that they could not be real followers of our perfect Islam and it was they who had corrupted its teachings. This "blame game" is still a big problem for Muslims, because they are quick to accuse other Muslims of fanaticism and terrorism without knowing that Islam itself promotes this very behavior, and it is this ignorance which causes violence and hostility between Islamic factions.

We were revolutionaries but our faith and minds were shaped by a royal culture that respected other beliefs and values. Iran (Persia) was the country of great kings who respected the beliefs of all tribes and nationalities in their kingdom and they left this legacy for Iranians to pass on from generation to generation. Prior to the Revolution no one imagined that

---

5   The party of Allah (*Hezbollah*) ... shall be triumphant (Q5:56).

other political parties would be suppressed under the rule of the Ayatollah Khomeini. He promised that all groups would have the freedom to run their own campaigns after the Revolution. He even stated that the governing system in Iran would be based on the decision of people by a referendum. He never spoke of a system that would be governed by Islam. He made it very clear that mullahs would take no part in politics: they would only be allowed to teach spirituality. The Ayatollah Khomeini knew that Iranians were an educated people who would not trust relatively uneducated mullahs. He kept his motives and plans well hidden knowing that he would lose the people's trust and confidence if he showed his true intentions, and possibly deny himself victory. Those mullahs in league with him never spoke against his statements before the Revolution, knowing he was working to deceive Iranians and the world.

The mullahs rushed into government offices occupying political positions immediately after the Revolution, making it difficult for the interim secular government to function. The interim prime minister, using an Iranian idiom, once said, "Ayatollah Khomeini entrusted the sword to us, but we have the handle of the sword, the edges are in the hands of mullahs." He was trying to say that the Ayatollah's colleagues acted as obstacles in his government, making it difficult for him to use his autonomy.

The mullahs' takeover of government positions was the opposite of what the Ayatollah Khomeini had promised to Iranians before the Revolution. Khomeini not only kept quiet but supported the mullahs' siege of the government, shocking many revolutionaries who trusted him. He exploited our zealous loyalty to himself and because of this he destroyed our trust in him and the mullahs surrounding him. As a result our hopes for a free Iran were dashed.

Why would a grand Muslim leader, the Ayatollah Khomeini, lie to millions? He was only doing as the Quran had instructed:

he was allowed to lie under certain circumstances[6] in order to gain power for the establishment of the real Islam.

Before the Revolution people thought the Ayatollah's entry to Iran would end 1400 years of conflict between Iranian and Saudi Arabian cultures. They also thought they would have the opportunity to serve their country as Iranians. But in reality he was secretly working to give priority to Muhammad's Arabian culture and language. His lies were a huge burden on Iranian Muslims who did not want to be yoked to Muhammad's seventh century nomadic culture. In 1400 years of battle, the Iranian culture lost little to Arabian culture. Now the Ayatollah Khomeini, a righteous Muslim, came with the most deceptive principles of Islam to put an end to the remnants of Iranian culture.

This became am issue of dispute among many Muslim revolutionaries: was our priority to be Iranian first or Muslim first? Like many others, I was caught in this dualistic war, struggling with what would be my identity, Iranian or Arabian. Should I be Iranian first and then Muslim or visa-versa? We wished the Ayatollah Khomeini would stay faithful in his promises to Iranians so that Iran would not stray away from its historical roots. His lies caused us to lose face among many Iranians who accepted our call to support the Ayatollah Khomeini prior to the Revolution.

Lack of experience and our busy revolutionary activities made us unable to evaluate whether or not the Ayatollah Khomeini would be able to lead us after the Revolution. We never imagined that his great success in leading the Revolution did not mean that he would be successful in leading the future government. We also did not realize that destroying a government was much easier than building it. We were driven to place our whole focus on overthrowing the rule of the Shah and capturing the

---

6   Q3:28; 2:225; 16:106; & *Reliance of the Traveller*, P.745. & *Dawud*, Book 14, Hadith 2498. & *Bukhari*, V. 3, B. 49, Hadith 857.

country. We had placed all eggs into the basket of learning the principles and practices of demolition and destruction. We did not have time to seek or evaluate the future or what principles were necessary for running a country. On the other hand we did not have practical experience of participatory leadership practically. Political leadership in the Middle-East was absolutely centralized because of Islam and obedience was absolute. We were obligated to leave every decision to our top leader. There were some people who criticized the Ayatollah Khomeini before the Revolution, challenging him with the accusation that did not have any plan for a future government. His response however was that everybody had to focus on the destruction of the Shah's regime and leave the future to the future. His entire focus was only to paralyze the monarchy in Iran and make his way to the top. His deceptive leadership and our blind obedience ultimately led the country to catastrophe after the Revolution.

With the tensions and uncertainties facing I decided that it was best to bide my time before rushing to join a particular side. My desire to make an educated decision led me to attend meetings to strengthen my knowledge of Islam. The Ayatollah Dr Morteza Motahhari was one of my favorite speakers and my frequent attendance at his lectures gave me the opportunity to ask him for a solution to the tensions among Muslim leaders. Motahhari hated the tensions among leaders, as it was going to diminish the power of revolutionaries against Israel and the West. He said that Rafsanjani, Beheshti, and Khamenei were three of the most dangerous of all mullahs and their intent was only to serve their thirst for power and their ambition would subvert Iran's Revolution. He also advised me to stay away from them. His advice confirmed my decision to hold off joining either side of the mullahs, even as tension between them grew daily.

A public referendum was held to decide between a ruling system, a republican system or some other form of government. Before the Revolution, the Ayatollah Khomeini told the people of Iran that whatever they decided, he would bow to it. To the astonishment of many, he did not stay faithful to his promises yet again, but insisted on the establishment of the "Islamic Republic of Iran" rather than only the "Republic of Iran". The addition of the word *Islamic* to the *Republic of Iran* meant that the country would be run under pure Islamic principles known as *Shari'a*, which does not give rights to any other Islamic or non-Islamic groups. Rights were to be given to Hezbollah only, the militia of Khomeini. This would be at the cost of all other groups and result in bloodshed. Under the *Shari'a* every group thinks of itself as the only legitimate group of Allah and of others as illegitimate, therefore, they must be destroyed. The history of these conflicts and bloodshed in Islam began immediately after the death of Muhammad when his in-laws sparked the Sunni movement and his son-in-law, the Shiite movement. Since that time radical followers of these two schools of Islam have been slaughtering each other in the name of their faith. Now, the history of Islam would repeat itself with the rise of Khomeini and the Islamic world was to witness bloodshed again.

6

Shari'a, the Law of Islam

The Mullahs Unveiled

Was it ever stated that the purpose of the Revolution was
a religious one and one that would empower the Ayatollah
Khomeini with authority to apply Shari'a law in Iran? Never.
The intention was supposedly a socio-political revolution that
would ensure the equal and just distribution of wealth among
Iranians by the vote of the people. Why would a righteous
Islamic leader change his mind and betray his nation? He did
it obviously to gratify his lust for power even at the cost of
his fellow Muslims and countrymen, aligning himself with
the political philosophy of Islam. Khomeini's manipulations
were so subtle and clever that it never occurred to the people
that he was deceiving them and the enforcement of Shari'a
established his absolute supremacy over every individual and
power in Iran. Even the elected president could not exercise
his own power without the supreme leader's approval.

The default on Khomeini's promises was the beginning of
unlimited persecution and bloodshed in Iran. His companion
mullahs in power killed even their own children, relatives and
friends who criticized them. The Ayatollah Shariatmadari,
who had millions of followers and had rescued the Ayatollah
Khomeini from the death penalty in 1963 under the rule of
the Shah, was imprisoned by the Ayatollah Khomeini himself.
Under his supremacy his own grandson was taken into

83

prison, and his own son died mysteriously. Great scholars and revolutionaries were humiliated, tortured, and murdered.

Before the Revolution we encouraged people to join the revolutionaries for a better Iran. We promised them that our situation would be far better than it had been under the Shah, but now we were embarrassed because of the Ayatollah Khomeini's betrayal since we had encouraged people to follow him for a democratic Iran. The freedom and opportunities under the Shah were not ideal but they were far more humane to what the Ayatollah Khomeini was offering to people.

Also, we, as committed Muslims, had wanted to unite our nation for the destruction of Israel and her ally America but we never wished to humiliate our own fellow citizens and create disunity. It had been encouraging to us that under the leadership of the Ayatollah Khomeini the revolutionaries were able to establish Hezbollah (the army of Allah) in Iran, and then in Lebanon as an extension and satellite of Iranian military intelligence to support the neighboring anti-Jews. Now, we worried that the internal disunity would hold us back in both our national and international goals.

We never knew that the mullahs would start with pro-democratic attitudes but demand absolute allegiance in the name of Islam later. We just did not see it coming. We did not know that they would hate Iranian culture and would enforce ancient Saudi Arabian culture to dominate the lives of Iranians. We were proudly calling ourselves Muslims, yet did not know that any disobedience to the mullahs would cost us our lives and our country. It never even entered our minds that the mullahs would slaughter even their own children for the sake of removing opposition.

The mullahs knew that in the long run they would not be able to lead Iranians for their cause because Iranians are rational people who love democracy. Therefore they did whatever it took to gain control over the country's weapons, wealth, business and every other thing to permanently silence any opposition. Their irrational thoughts and disorderly actions created economic chaos and the gap between rich and poor became wider and wider. They ignored the desperate need of the nation but invested billions of dollars for the sake of terrorism via Syria in order to strengthen anti-Israeli militias in Lebanon and Palestine. The poor were quickly forgotten.

The mullahs who had once spoken harshly against a luxurious lifestyle now admired it. Though poverty prevailed everywhere in the country, the mullahs became rich and lascivious. They were blaming people for their poverty, saying that a person would not be poor if he or she obeyed the Ayatollah Khomeini wholeheartedly. I remember the day the Ayatollah Shabestari, a close companion of the Ayatollah Khomeini, visited a northern city in Iran and passed through our city. The local mullah in power asked him to make a short stop in our city so the Ayatollah Khomeini's zealous followers could send their greeting to him via his close friend. He stopped in the biggest mosque in town. Both the men and women's sections of the mosque were packed full. Among many other questions, one particular question was directed to him by a young mother. She was crying and said to him that her family did not have enough food and therefore she was weak and unable to produce milk for her newborn baby. She also did not have money to buy powder milk to feed her baby. To the astonishment of all he raised his voice loudly and repeatedly the saying, "We have the Ayatollah Khomeini as our leader in this country, that means we are rich". This was the response to a young mother who was worrying about her child and pouring out her tears for the hunger threatening the life of her new baby.

The mullahs' contempt for people was obvious in every aspect of life. Some of them raped younger girls and boys who were sent to them to learn the Quran. A day did not go by that a mullah did not rape a child. Girls who tried to refuse them were accused baselessly, imprisoned, tortured and even killed. If a girl opposed the mullahs' rule and received the death sentence and she was a virgin the mullahs raped her before killing her. This was so that she would fall into the category of an infidel sex-slave (concubine), so under Islamic law her murder would not be a sin.

Men who opposed the mullahs were imprisoned, humiliated by every kind of unethical word, tortured and killed. The mullahs had a license to utter any unethical and immoral word and do whatever they liked with the prisoners. No one was able to criticize them anymore. Criticism of them was interpreted as criticism of Muhammad and Allah, and the penalty was death[1]. One mullah, the Ayatollah Hassani, who was also a judge, killed his own two sons because they opposed the Ayatollah Khomeini.

I decided to leave Tehran and go to my hometown, where there was no political or religious tension yet. I thought that, away from Tehran I could perhaps do something for my nation and stay faithful to our promises to the people. I could serve and encourage them so together we could raise our country to democracy and to a better future. I needed to focus more on serving people than involving myself in struggle for power. I also wanted to prove that as a member of the Revolution I could be true to my promises. I was also ready to speak out against the tensions and discrimination imposed by the mullahs in Tehran if I was asked.

I began my ministry by teaching younger people that the communist belief of our northern neighbor, Russia, was baseless compared to religious philosophy that believed in God and the creation. I believed this would encourage them to stand against the spread of communism and Russian influence in Iran and attach themselves strongly to Islam. This also gave me an opportunity to unite the younger people to help them prepare themselves for rebuilding our country with Islamic values, spreading Islam internationally, and for aiding the Palestinians and the Shiite militias against Israel in the future.

---

1   Q8:12-13; 33:36.

I worked hard to attract younger people to engage themselves in my teachings and to attend camps where fighting, terrorist and suicide bombing techniques were taught.

Finding My Soul Mate

It was during these activities that I met my wife. She loved to be a channel for the spread of fundamentalism at home and abroad. Her major interest in Islam began when she was eighteen years old, just before the 1979 Revolution, when the Ayatollah Khomeini entered Iran after years of exile. Due to her father's disinterest in Islam her family was not practicing Islam, even by nominal standards. He was an atheist who ran away from the Russian State of Azerbaijan to Iran in the time of Stalin (who killed non-communists as well as communist opponents). He could never manifest his atheist belief in Iran openly, since the Shah of Iran was pro-West and anti-communist. However, towards the last months of the Shah's reign, when he was losing his power to the revolutionaries, my wife's father took part in the street protests. This was partly because the Revolution was more socially and politically motivated and Iranian communists could identify with it.

Daniel finds his soul mate

My wife also went to the protests with her father, gradually showing interest in the Revolution and deciding to become a follower of the Ayatollah Khomeini. She was influenced by the comparative courses and consequently decided to support the Revolution as an Islamic religious person.

I met my wife for the first time in one of my comparative courses. Her regular attendance and our common interests led to my interest in her and we soon married. We did not know each other personally. It was illegal for a boy and girl to get together, talk about their personalities or families, and plan for life to see whether there was enough common ground for unity in marriage. Dating is totally forbidden. It was also illegal for me to express my desire directly to her or receive her consent. However, contrary to common practice, I secretly gave a letter to her asking her to be my wife. She shared this with her parents and they allowed her to respond positively.

The main reason she married was to uphold the traditions of Islam which forbids young women from remaining single. She was also determined to attach herself to a radical Muslim man so that she could fight for Islam side by side by him and release herself from the limitations of ancient Islamic marriage which requires women to stay at home.[2] If they wanted to go out they had to cover themselves in a way so that nobody could distinguish who they were.[3] Since this was against the Iranian culture for women, she wanted to remain an Iranian Muslim too, encouraging many other younger girls to stay closer to Islam.

Against Iranian custom, our marriage was performed in a mosque. The mosque was a symbol to our followers of the importance of Islam. If we wanted Iranians to be radical Muslims our whole lives had to be centered on Islam, and the mosque itself was preeminent in our beliefs. Our marriage

---

2   Q33:33.

3   Q33:59-61.

motivated many younger girls to attach themselves more closely to Islam.

A mosque, in addition to being a place of worship is also a court, a military garrison, and a parliament for committed Muslims to prepare themselves in every aspect for fighting non-Muslims or any infidelity among Muslims. Committed Muslims are obligated to fight non-Muslims and all who oppose them, even those who are their relatives.[4] A mosque is the best place for them to learn hatred towards their opposition and non-Muslims. Muhammad, the prophet of Islam, taught hatred to his followers in his own mosque and then led them to destroy the Jewish city of Medina.[5]

The mosque is also vital for establishing Muslims as sovereign over non-Muslims in a non-Islamic society. Building a mosque in a non-Islamic society or country symbolizes Islam's claim over that society or country, even with a non-Muslim majority. The Quran states that all lands belong to Muslims even if they have never occupied them.[6] Once Islam assumes power over the government, non-Muslim citizens will be given a choice to join Islam or be killed. Non-Muslims may also buy their lives yearly in order to be spared a death penalty, but only if they are Jews or Christians.[7] When Islam rules over a country Muslims become the real citizens and owners of that country and non-Muslims fall into a second class citizenship that is unequal to Muslims.[8]

By having our marriage ceremony in a mosque my wife and I wanted to teach our followers to understand the significance of the mosque in the spread of Islam. Our marriage attracted the attention of many people. As revolutionaries we planned

---

4   Q9:123.

5   *Bukhari*, Volume 9, Book 92, Hadith 447. & *Bukhari*, Volume 4, Book 53, Hadith 392. & *Muslim*, Book 19, Hadith 4363.

6   Q33:27.

7   Q9: 5, 28-30.

8   Q3:110.

to send some of our followers to non-Islamic countries in the near future with the primary mission of gathering Muslim support and build mosques. We needed to build a foundation for people to learn the role of mosque. Many Islamic countries have invested millions of dollars in non-Islamic countries to build mosques and Islamic schools which helps to pave the way for Muslims to own those countries. Building a mosque in a non-Islamic country is a seal of ownership for committed and radical Muslims.

Muhammad's Initiatives: My Motive

I won the trust of many young people in my hometown and helped them prepare for two wars or jihads. The first jihad was against poverty and the second against Israel and the West, especially America. Muhammad had also two jihadi initiatives. These two jihadi steps were his main approaches to Islamization of the societies around him. He promised his followers a prosperous life and planned to provide for their needs so they would follow him. With mostly poor followers, Muhammad was unable to establish a strong army for Islam. He decided to use wives, concubines and slaves as the center of his plans for the spread of Islam. He needed great wealth for his plans, which was more important to him than anything else, so he legalized the looting of non-Muslims since there was no other income source for him. He and his small community began looting the caravans of pagan Meccans and thus obtained great wealth. His community prospered and he was able to hire more followers as a result. His number of soldiers grew and he was able to establish a strong army. Without this army he could not have invaded the Jewish tribes in Medina or the pagans in Mecca putting an end to their history on the peninsula of Arabia.

We also needed to follow his footsteps as followers of Muhammad in Iran and do the same with the zealous Iranian Muslims but with contemporary tools. We didn't need to loot non-Muslims; our country sat on rich oil fields and had great income from selling oil. We believed we could strengthen our followers with oil money, gaining access to most advanced weapons and dominate other societies. However, the Ayatollah Khomeini and his surrounding mullahs did not have the same politico-religious mind as Muhammad. Khomeini ignored his Iranian followers while supporting Syria, Hezbollah in Lebanon and the Palestinians against Israel. He did not see a need to strengthen his Iranian followers first. I knew he would not be able to quicken the destruction of Israel by ignoring his own nation. Instead he would rather be the cause of hatred and bloodshed in his own country.

Iran was not a radical Islamic country when the Ayatollah Khomeini became the supreme leader. The Revolution's purpose was not to turn Iranians into radical Muslims. Many Iranians who rejected the rule of the Shah were nominal Muslims. The revolutionaries desired freedom and economic and political justice. Their minds were far from the idea that Islam had to be carried world-wide, or that Israel and America had to be destroyed. Only the Ayatollah Khomeini and his very close companions knew that they had to change the direction of the Revolution secretly and progressively. Even the real followers of the Ayatollah Khomeini, including myself, who only made up even less than 2 per cent of the entire Iranian community, did not know his plan for the future. What we heard clearly was that the Shah had to leave Iran; as long as the Shah remained people could not have their rights. It was later that we were gradually persuaded that Islam must rule.

So we, Khomeini's followers, needed to spend money and find many followers. Without committed followers we would not be able to reach our goal of destroying America or Israel. Khomeini obtained power but did not have a long-term plan for Islam. Not only did he not have a plan, he did not have capability to develop one. His initiatives became very random. He invaded the American Embassy in Tehran without knowing that Iranians were not ready to fight America yet.

Like the Ayatollah Khomeini and his surrounding mullahs, we also hated America and Israel. Hostility to America and Israel was the central pillar of radical Muslims goals. But we wanted to have a strong Muslim nation first, establishing a strong Islamic economy like Saudi Arabia, and then we would start our international mission. That would prepare the ground for us to employ cultural, political and economic jihadists to penetrate and undermine western values from inside and destroy them. We believed Israel could not be captured without paralyzing America. An Israel without America would be like a piece of bread for us to swallow.

Hometown Hero

Like Muhammad, I began the fight against poverty in my Muslim nation to prepare them for the real jihad against

non-Muslims. People living in my hometown told me that the work I did in my hometown in one year was more than the mullahs accomplished in the 30 years of their rule in the region. I established an organization called *Building Jihad*, to construct roads and schools in rural areas and take electricity to many villages and giving residents access to the advantages of bigger cities.

My actions proved that I was not like the mullahs in Tehran, who only wanted to fill their own pockets, ignored the poverty of their own people and rushed into terrorism. My service in the area

Daniel praying to Allah in 1981

made me famous, which eventually led to my candidacy for the Islamic parliament.

The first election for the newly established Islamic parliament was drawing close. By this time I had many followers and was beginning to lead them like a party which was distinct from what the mullahs had established. The mullahs didn't want any other party or movement, and the Quran rejects a multitude of parties. "Only the party of Allah *(Hezbollah)* must triumph."[9] For this reason, there is always struggle in fundamentalist Islamic countries among parties. Sunnis, the followers of Muhammad's in-laws, and Shiites, the followers of his son-in-law, have slaughtered millions of each other's people since the death of Muhammad because of political differences. Islam is a political and military religion and, as a result, every sect or group of Islam is to at least some extent both political and military. Every group believes that the other groups cannot be real Muslims or of the party of Allah, and that they therefore must be destroyed. Because of this the Ayatollah Khomeini and his friends decided to destroy other parties.

After a while, I discovered that many revolutionaries in other parts of the country had achieved some success with the same political philosophy I had, and had acquired many followers. This gave me hope that we could be the majority in parliament in the near future and would be able to lead the country with a practical Islamic plan toward the future. Alas, I was not aware that the mullahs would do whatever it took in order to push back servant leaders and take their own proteges to the parliament.

To Israel and Beyond

The organization of Building Jihad grew rapidly with many activities and areas of expertise. My fame led many people to commit themselves to Islam and to follow my plan. There is a strong political voice of Islam that says, "Muslims must first

---

9   Q5:56.

Daniel while preparing young people for war against Israel and the West in 1981

establish power and then use their power to spread Islam. A powerful Muslim community must always have the Quran in one hand and a sword in the other for fighting and imposing Islam." This saying is the daily bread of fanatic Muslims everywhere. This was always the concluding message of my speeches in mosques or public places in my hometown. Our goal was to overcome the enemy at home first, any enemy that was an obstacle to the prosperity of people, and then take Islam abroad to establish an Islamic Empire (the Caliphate).

Our emphatic international goal was to capture Israel, eradicate all Jews, and make Israel a capital state for all Islamic nations, handing over its government to our Shiite brothers (the future members of Hezbollah) in Lebanon. To make our people believe in our movement and be part of our international goal we influenced them psychologically (for example by removing existing road signs and replacing them with signs pointing to Israel). Signs indicating 500 or 1000 kilometers to Tehran were replaced with the signs showing 2000 or so kilometers to Israel. We had to first put the belief in the minds and hearts of people that Jews do not have any land rights in the Middle-East. All lands belong to Muslims and the Muslim world.

Saddam's Interference

To achieve our goal for Israel, we first needed to overthrow Saddam Hussein's regime in Iraq. Even though we had separated ourselves from the mullahs, like the mullahs we too believed that Saddam had to go. Our message to Iranians was that to invade Israel we had to first overthrow Saddam's government. Saddam was not only a nominal Muslim dictator; he was also a Sunni, who ignored the rights of Shiites in Iraq, torturing and killing them. We believed that the majority Shiites needed to rule over Iraq, which would be our highway to Israel. We began to establish a government for Iraq in Iran, appointing the Ayatollah Hakim, an Iraqi Shiite clergy, as the head of that government. Our plan became urgent after Saddam invaded Iran. His invasion was a good excuse for the Ayatollah Khomeini to retaliate. He hated Saddam and aimed to destroy his regime. Then the Ayatollahs hated the goals of Sunni Saddam and his Baath party, which was to capture and unify Islamic countries under the umbrella of his party.

The invasion of Saudi Arabia was also part of our plan, but it was a second priority. Our major focus was to capture Iraq first. After that, our leaders believed that if Shiites captured Saudi Arabia, especially Mecca, then they would be able to stop the growth of Sunni doctrine progressively and spread the Shia faith everywhere.

7

War: A Good Excuse

War broke out between Iraq and Iran and expanded rapidly. Saddam's invasion was a good excuse for the Ayatollah Khomeini to fulfill his agenda concerning Iraq. We did not know that he would also use the war as an excuse to destroy those who were not in favor of his country policy. He used the excuse that the country was at war and any criticism to him would weaken the voice of the true Islam, Shia, and strengthen the voice of the Sunni enemy Saddam, Israel and the West.

Interestingly, Iranian and Iraqi leaders accused each other of being the Zionist agents in order to justify their invasions and stir their people psychologically against each other until the final goal was obtained, which was the occupation and destruction of Iran for Saddam and the occupation and destruction of Iraq for the Ayatollah Khomeini.

The war became a golden opportunity for the mullahs to fight Saddam. It seemed like the prey coming to the hunter. Even when Saddam requested a cease fire and peace after some months the Ayatollah Khomeini rejected his request. He said that he could not have peace with the enemy of Islam; "Peace with an enemy is like drinking poison," he said. He twisted words in order to avoid peace and show himself as a righteous hero. After eight years of bloodshed, and the death of over a million from both Iran and Iraq, the Ayatollah agreed to a peace treaty with Saddam. This time also he tried to show himself as a hero again but in a different way. He likened his peace with Saddam to "drinking poison" and said that he had no choice but to drink that poison and avoid bloodshed. Some of his followers cried out, praising his humility in harming himself by drinking that so-called poison. They were too blinded to remember his twisted comments when he said at the beginning of the war that he could not drink the poison of a peace treaty with Saddam.

We knew that Saddam was a bully. He had once breached Iran's border in the time of the Shah but the Shah taught him a lesson. This time also, it was he who invaded Iran first and for this reason many Iranians, including a great number of those in opposition, believed that Saddam had to be punished: the Iranian armed forces had to fight his army and force them back. However, Khomeini cleverly turned the war into a religious war, the war of righteous ones against infidels. He tried whatever he could and used every form of religious art in order to move people religiously and receive their support for the occupation of Iraq. Many committed Muslims supported his plan and sent their sons, even the younger ones, to war. Almost all of these younger boys lacked army skills. For this reason, many of them died. They were used mainly to show how big the army of Islam was. Before sending them to the war zones, the mullahs asked them to wear head bandanas of martyrdom, and declare in street meetings that they were the real followers of Muhammad, ready to fight and die for Islam.

During the war, Building Jihad was forced to curtail many activities and support the war effort. The president Banisadr was still in Iran and the second chief commander in charge of the war, after Khomeini, according to the law. I served on the front lines, not as fighter but in logistics, and avoided death on numerous occasions. My younger brother and my brother-in-law were both injured as fighting soldiers. The war resulted in more than a million dead, disabled and injured Iranians.

A Candidate for the Islamic Parliament

Since the second year after the Revolution, many non-clerical Muslim politicians like me had kept their distance from the vile mullahs and their political party, the Islamic Republican Party. The party was called the Republican Party but did not have anything to do with the republic. Its aim was absolute dominance and we were highly disappointed in its policy. The Party's overriding goal was to support the Shiite militias in Lebanon, the Sunni militias in Palestine, and the anti-Semitic Syrian government to conquer Israel. The needs of the public were therefore secondary to the Party. We established our own political groups or independent communities.

A candidate for the Islamic Parliament, and an opposition Member in 1981

I had prepared myself and was ready to announce my candidacy for the Islamic parliament as an independent candidate. The leader of the Islamic Republican Party in our state, Dr Hassan-e Azodi, was aware of my reputation in the area and therefore urged me to return to the Republican party and become their candidate for the parliament. But I refused. There was to be a meeting of the Islamic Republican Party delegates in Tehran and he urged me for the second time to go with him to attend the meeting, hoping that the meeting would change my mind and I would become a supporter of the mullahs. I declined his offer. Dr Azodi went without me. The meeting ended tragically when a bomb blast killed many attendees, including Dr Azodi.

Eventually, I announced my candidacy as an independent. The public had seen the dirty games of the Islamic Republican Party and were interested in independent candidates. The first Islamic president, Dr Abulhassan Banisadr also ran as an independent and won the election with around 80 per cent of the people's vote, a proof that many Iranians were fed up with the mullahs. I was more of a follower of Banisadr's political philosophy than of Khomeini's and the mullahs. Dr Banisadr was more liberal in his approach and respected the rights of others.

The Mullahs' Bitter Attitudes

My refusal of the Islamic Republican Party's offer resulted in the mullahs' bitter attitudes toward me. When they saw that they had lost their credibility with the people they sought to retain power through any means possible. Tricks, creating confusion, threats, bullying and attacks became their daily practices to dominate and stop the opposition. They hired street boys, gangs, ex-aristocrats and their children, and gave them overt money and weapons to create anarchy and serve them with their best. In creating chaos the mullahs disregarded the rights of the interim government run by Mr Bazargan and ultimately gained control over all cities. The government was not in their hands officially but they acquired all army artillery which gave them the power. Later on, several times they plotted to kill the president, Dr Banisadr. Finally, he, who had won the election with 80 per cent of people's vote, fled and took refuge in France.

The elected president of the people was forced to escape and his government was demolished. Life for the mullahs' opponents became unbearable after the escape of the president. Backed by the Ayatollah Khomeini, the mullahs took control of the government and ordered their followers to openly humiliate and beat us in the streets, the market places, our work places and even in our houses. They invaded homes in the middle of the night and terrorized our families. I was harassed and beaten by their revolutionary guards many times in the streets. On one occasion they gave a rifle to one of my followers, ordering him to kill me. They said if he refused to kill me they would kill his children and destroy his family.

It was the middle of the night when we heard someone knocking at our door. When I opened the door, I saw my friend and co-worker pointing a rifle at me. With astonishment, I asked, "What is the matter? What is this in your hand?" He cried and refused to kill me. He said that his children's lives were in danger if he did not kill me. Though terrified, I told him to shoot me and rescue his children. The sobbing man refused. "I cannot do this," he said. I pulled him inside and we discussed a solution. He decided to go back to his home, get his wife and children, and leave the city immediately. The mullahs were doing this to their opponents in order to compel them to join their party and serve their cause.

Parliament Election

It was not possible for me to run away despite the threats and persecution. I had already submitted my candidacy for the parliament and everybody was aware of it. Culturally, it would bring shame to me if I ran and ignored the trust put in me by my people, especially when I saw that people were behind me despite threats. They were all hoping their votes would change current conditions. They hoped to teach a lesson to the mullahs, that they had no place in their hearts and no choice but to leave power to the people.

The mullahs were also hoping that through pressure they would be able to frighten people and force them to give up supporting us.

The aristocrats of the area advised the leader of the Islamic Republican Party to nominate a cleric for the parliament who had been in their service for years before the Revolution. The Islamic Republican Party was searching for support from every faction and therefore accepted their advice and nominated a mullah who wanted to get rid of me at any cost.

I received a threat from his followers that if I went out of my house on the day of election, they would shoot me. They already had marked those who were my supporters and attacked them in the voting areas.

The mullahs' philosophy was that they were the only ordained people of Allah (Hezbollah in Arabic) and they had to overcome opposition at any cost.[1] They therefore were striving to eradicate all of us. They used whatever it took to paralyze our organizations. They even used these tactics on their own family members who supported other parties or independent candidates.

The mullahs did what it took to control the election and prevent other candidates from entering parliament. The guards and the mullahs' representatives threw many boxes containing votes into a river in my hometown, keeping only those boxes that held the majority votes for them. Eventually they got their own candidate into the parliament.

Visiting Khomeini

My followers and I decided to visit the Ayatollah Khomeini, to communicate to him the injustices done to us by the mullahs and to plead with him for counsel and help. We collected documents, proofs of the fraudulent election, and headed for Tehran. We were hoping that the Ayatollah Khomeini would listen to us and act justly. But we were denied a meeting with him and told he was not well. We were referred to the Ayatollah Imami Jamarani, who was housing the Ayatollah Khomeini and assured that Jamarani would take our message to Khomeini.

---

1   Q5:56.

We showed Jamarani the documents and explained the injustices of the mullahs in our city. Jamarani was aware of the crimes and angry with the top Republican Party mullahs. He said that they treated the Ayatollah Khomeini like a remote control to get whatever they wanted. They passed their messages and plans to people through the mouth of the Ayatollah Khomeini, using or abusing his supreme position in order to make their words and plans receivable by people. He said that Khomeini had no choice but to convey their commands. Behind the curtain they were the leaders, not Khomeini. They worked through Khomeini because he was still the leader in the people's mind and it wasn't time for the surrounding mullahs to get rid of him yet. He told us quietly and with clear words, "You have a hard and dangerous task ahead. Unfortunately without their confirmation, Khomeini cannot listen to you."

Some members of our convoy became terrified when they discovered the mullahs had nailed down their dictatorship and there was no hope for anyone to stand up for their rights unless they were pro-mullahs. Back home, many of these friends reduced their relationship with me and eventually lived as strangers to me in order to survive.

Shortly after the entry of my parliamentarian competitor, the Ayatollah Younes-e Erfani, three of his clergy friends were appointed as judges in the Revolutionary Supreme Court ruling over many cities, the judge of our city's Revolutionary Court, and the Supreme Religious Authority (*Imam Jum'a*, who represented the Ayatollah Khomeini and led the Friday prayers) over our city. One of his young ruthless guards also was appointed as the Revolutionary Mayor over the city. These four people made life hell for me, depriving me of the right to work or gain money for my family. I could either continue as their opposition and endure a painful life, or bow down and make myself their slave. I made my decision, knowing it could mean death: I would not succumb to their threats.

The hardship I faced at the hands of these Muslim brothers gradually exposed the true values of Islamic political philosophy to me and many others. People were shocked at how badly oppositions and political prisoners were treated. Still, some of us did not want to lose hope of freedom since it was still the early years of the Islamic style government. We were ready to pay the cost of freedom by exposing the deceits of the ruling mullahs. The mullahs were also trying to establish their absolute authoritarian leadership at any cost, using references from the Quran and Muhammad's sayings to persuade people that Islam could not be established without force.[2] Allah has ordained Muslims to be harsh.[3]

Khomeini's Silence

The Ayatollah Khomeini kept silent about the injustices of the Republican Party mullahs. We, the democratic front, still hoped to win over the country and rule by our own type of Islamic justice. In our minds we falsely held on to the idea that the Ayatollah Khomeini would stand for the democratic leadership of Dr Banisadr and would not praise the mullahs who thirst for dictatorship. We thought that his silence did not mean agreement with the mullahs, but that he was acting as a patient father who would soon stop their destruction. Our view was strengthened when Khomeini's own son, a cleric living with him, expressed support for Dr Banisadr's leadership by speaking against the Republican Party mullahs.

There were also other renowned and influential clerics who were Khomeini's supporters and longtime friends who spoke against these mullahs. We had hope that he would one day break his silence in favor of us. Though Khomeini's silence was strange and unbearable we had no choice but to wait. We took it as a gesture of Iranian paternalistic culture that encourages children to wait and parents to stand up, break the silence and say to his rebellious children, "Enough is enough, stop it."

---

2 Q33:36; 8:10-13.

3 Q9:123.

Though we were impatient for the arrival of such a moment, we never thought that our cries and criticisms would be ignored. We believed he would eventually break his so-called fatherly silence and him stand up for us against the abusive mullahs. If that happened he would have received much appreciation and praise for helping the well-being of his country.

Alas, his silence became an omen of death to us and all those in opposition and a sign of destruction for the whole country. His silence resulted in humiliation, imprisonment and the death sentence for many of us, including his own son and grandson. His silence was part of a plot that only became clear when it was too late for us to fight our false father. We never suspected that he and his surrounding mullahs would sanction the death of even their own children for the convenience of Islamic authoritarian politics.

The Ayatollah Khomeini's deceptive silence sprang from the Islamic doctrine of *taqiyya* (legitimate deceiving), nurtured under the wings of an evil spirit which was waiting for the right moment to transform Iran into a Shari'a compliant Islamist state. This Shari'a transformation would destroy the social and political promises of the Revolution and turn it into a bastion of Islamic terrorism against Iranians, Israel, the West and all infidels. Khomeini was waiting for the right moment to reveal his radical Islamic totalitarianism to aid in the destruction of all groups who hoped for freedom.

In those moments of silence, Khomeini's surrounding mullahs knew that he was waiting for them to subtly create more division among the democratic voices. They worked to disable the democratic groups in every possible way, to make it easier to establish their own unified front. They succeeded because no opposition group was able to unite with other opposition groups. The mullahs saw the ground was ready for a takeover and immediately rushed from the shadows of manipulation into the corridors of full power. They captured everything and then marched openly to extinguish the democratic voices. First, they aimed at President Banisadr's position and life.

As a result, Banisadr had no choice but to flee the country. After this, one by one those in opposition were targeted by the power-seeking mullahs. Some of those in opposition were able to leave the country, but many were unable to escape. They were killed or given life imprisonment or were forced to compromise.

The Establishment of Shari'a

The mullahs used stealth and intrigue to seize complete power in various government offices. This also gained them many followers. Then they steered their people to raise their voice in favor of Shari'a establishment in every place, so everything could be ruled according to the Islamic principles.

To turn around the country's culture and make it theocratic, the mullahs elevated religious leadership above everything else, so nobody had the right to speak out against their words and decisions. Eventually they established Shari'a and began to terrify people with implementing slashing and death sentences in streets and squares. People were gripped with fear. Even leftists who did not believe in any religion started to bow down to the mullahs and act religious because of the unbearable persecutions. One of my old friends who held a high position in a significant government office told me one day that he saw Mr Ehsan Tabari, a renowned Iranian communist leader, praying the Islamic daily prayer in a famous prison in Tehran.

When the bubble of Islamic holy deception (*taqiyya*) burst, many of our fellow citizens discovered that it was too late to fight the mullahs or stay away from them. People suddenly discovered that the path of vicious radicalism was set wider than any other way. They had to decide whether to side with the mullahs and live, or stay away and be deprived of everything or die. The fear of destruction overshadowed everyone. Not many dared to take a look at their situation and ask themselves how and in what way their decisions would shape their and their country's future life. They were not able to think strategically but rather took refuge under the unethical wings of the mullahs and made the destruction of Iran their daily agenda.

Many pro-democratic Iranians broke down morally and gave up courage because of the mullahs' ferocious use of terror. Some were gradually absorbed into the regime to avoid social and political deprivations. Furthermore, they started to ay that they were wrong about the mullahs and had now found truth. Instead they were working with them to uproot the remnants of western culture in Iran. They themselves started to preach what they had once called a foolish doctrine, blaming supporters of democracy with words like "Zionist," "Western Agent," etc, torturing us emotionally.

Things changed shockingly for the worse. Even many of my friends, who were once victims of dictatorship and loyal advocates of freedom, joined the mullahs and functioned as the hands and legs of Islamic dictatorship, shooting their zeal for freedom in the foot. Some of these so-called champions of freedom undertook the role of spying for the mullahs and others became persecutors of freedom fighters in prison. One of my humble followers was appointed as the head of the prison, viciously persecuting and torturing opponents. Many others also were enthralled by superstitious Islamic commands which encouraged them to follow the mullahs blindly, as Muhammad the prophet of Islam had commanded: "Striving in the path of Allah (*jihad*) is incumbent on you along with every ruler, whether he is pious or impious; ..."[4]. Since the Ayatollah Khomeini was related to Muhammad genealogically, nobody could say or even imagine that he had an impiety in his life. The only choice was to follow him blindly. So, the quality of leadership was not an issue for many people anymore, but what Islam said and conditions dictated.

Many of our young people who were once shouting for democracy in the streets of Iran and were ready to give

---

4   *Dawud*, Book 14, Hadith 2527.

their lives for it, were now employed to impose the mullah's authoritarianism over their nation at every level of life. Some were also encouraged to join Muslim militias in Lebanon and Palestine to fight against Israel. The ground was progressively prepared so everybody felt obligated forcefully to fight the mullahs' opponents, or otherwise face persecution.

After the mullahs seized power they also seized all pro-monarchist and western businesses and forced the expatriates out. The country became disconnected from the outside world although it was still dependent upon foreign products on many levels. It fell into a great economic recession. The economic depression also made many people needy and more vulnerable to the mullah's influence. The mullahs started to blame the West, Israel and the democratic front for the country's shortages.

Nearly every day in the cities, the mullahs gathered their chanting followers in the streets to blame America and Israel for the problems of the country and show the opposition that they had people's support. People in government offices, schools, and universities who received salaries from the government were forced to join the street propaganda meetings.

The mullahs turned schools, universities, hospitals and all public places into religious-political centers. They Islamized every aspect of life. Their morality was low wherever they stepped foot because the words of the Quran says that the righteous followers of Allah had to act harshly.[5] Fear shadowed the public. Close relatives and friends whispered in each other's ears: *Divar moosh darad, Moosh goosh darad*, which means the wall has a mouse; the mouse has ears. In other words: watch your tongue, don't even trust your family members since subtle deceptions are hard to distinguish. We, therefore, were no longer able to speak about our rights to anyone except to whisper in the ears of those few friends who

---

5   Q9:123.

still had secret courage and desired the rule of the mullahs to fade away.

On the cultural front life went downhill and thousands of younger people left their heritage and were absorbed to the Revolutionary Guard (*Sepah*) and to the Correcting Religious Guard (*Basijis*). These were established to Islamize the country and make sure that everybody lived according to Islamic principles. What was envisioned before the Revolution as prosperity and creativity now became a lifestyle for many to persecute fellow citizens. These younger religious guards were led by the mullahs to torture and kill people in public places. They wanted to terrify people and extinguish any desire for opposition, thus gaining more power.

The mullahs used economic downturn, unemployment and poverty as a means to gain power and rule endlessly. Under the garment of morality, they did whatever they could in order to justify their violence in the name of Islamic rule and establish their despotism. People who cared for their culture and country, started to think that their best days were left in the past, the kingdom of the Shah, but it was too late.

The mullahs also used the widespread and traditional choice slogans of Antisemitism as a strong weapon for misleading the masses. They wanted to establish themselves as the legitimate Islamic rulers who have authority from Allah to destroy Israel. Any opposition was marked with the demonized words of 'Jew' or 'American' and eventually crushed. The Mullahs hated a western style freedom and patiently waited with their tyrannical principles for years until they could enslave us.

Because of fear, people had to be ready to sing the song of "Down with America and Israel" anytime the mullahs wanted to protests in the streets. If a business did not close for protests then the owner could be blamed with the words "Zionist" or "Western Spy." The mullahs created an atmosphere where everybody was pro-mullah, anti-America and anti-Israel.

The mullahs left us only two options; to rescue ourselves from their humiliations, discrimination and attacks, or to surrender ourselves to their tyrannical leadership and join others in torturing opponents and our nation. A few opponents, who struggled to stomach such an allegiance, chose to be humiliated rather than humiliating others. But many joined the mullahs.

It was a painful experience for me to see to what extent the courage of my democratically-minded fellow citizens failed them, and fell short of preserving their nation's right and prestige. Worse yet, they, who once showed intelligence and cried for freedom, now chose to cast their votes for an oppressive regime, and surrendered their birthright of freedom of their children and grandchildren in exchange for the mullahs' favor.

One of my followers was one of my persecutors when I was later taken to prison. Many others like him saw the mullahs' bloodiest commands as legitimate and called their actions righteousness. Because of fear, people started to stay away from opponents of the regime. They did not want to risk their families. Under the authoritarian and self-centered Islamic government our society's moral characters diminished and some got paid for persecuting of others, causing people to forget that they needed to uphold and take care of each other. Because of this, our beautiful country fell into the hands of a power-thirsty sect which saw every other thing as secondary, including national coherence.

The mullahs were living their best days. These religious tyrants followed the humiliating philosophy of Islam[6] and made savvy use of proxy gangsters, criminals and terrorists to handcuff people and push them further and further behind, truly impacting the country negatively for generations to come.

The media also fell into the hands of the mullahs. They stopped reporting anything irrelevant to the mullahs and censored

6   Q58:20.

every idea that was contrary to their way of thinking. They were used as the most influential channels for authorizing Shair'a to dominate every area of life, allowing things which were once a disdain to Iranian culture. They loudly and proudly announced the blood-thirsty culture of Muhammad superior over Iranian culture. They wanted to eradicate national identity and dress with hostile Meccan culture. Sometimes, they spoke in favor of Iranian identity but such statements were only for public consumption.

Blind obedience became the channel for the Ayatollah Khomeini to claim to be ruling in Muhammad's place. People believed him and forgot the pride of our nation that sheltered tolerance and protected the rights of everybody, no matter what race, religion and color. They sadly poured their Persian identity under the feet of the Ayatollah and the mullahs, and offered up our beautiful country as a nest to terrorism.

Now, we hear and read that thousands of the children of those blinded fellows in Iran are protesting for freedom in the streets and many get slaughtered by tyrannical mullahs every year. They bullied, humiliated and destroyed our lives without thinking that the dictator mullahs will also destroy their own children in the future.

I was often bullied and mocked by younger religious guards in the street. I witnessed and experienced how these younger followers of the mullahs shouted catcalls and curses in the streets after humiliating us and fell over one another to cheer their victory. The most humiliating part was that some of these younger fellows were my own relatives. It is so sad to see that the children of revolutionaries are suffering now from a regime to which their parents dedicated their lives.

Before the Revolution, we could not imagine that the day would come to our country when we would be humiliated by those who were claiming to be pro-democracy. The mullahs fought with us, claiming they wanted to end authoritarianism in Iran forever. However their own regime became more despotic and unethical than the Shah's and than any other regime since the dominance of Islam in Iran.

We were shocked, confused and frustrated. We felt crushed under the mullahs' subtle deceptions (Islamic *taqiyya*). Once we had striven for the Iranian dream but then surrendered to despair and destruction.

The pressures people faced were so great and they stopped listening to our cries. The hostility of the mullahs towards western investors led the country into economic crisis, slowing down manufacturing activity, causing job losses, escalating gas prices and causing food shortages. People struggled just to live and had nothing left in them to care about the mullah's destructive plans.

The mullahs took over big businesses and made them governmental. They did not listen to experts but appointed people on the top of the organization who did not have any organizational skills. Experts who did not agree with them were sacked and forced to leave the country. Blind obedience and allegiance surpassed the quality of work and life. As a result, the economy failed and the distribution of everything became subject to coupons. People had to wait hours and days in lines in order to get rice, eggs, and their other daily needs. The mullahs said that they rather die in hunger than have a relationship with the West. They wished to seize the wealth of the West rather than growing wealth through a friendly relationship with them.

Unemployment increased, the nation lost its purchasing power and started to suffer through all aspects of life. Poverty and struggle to find food changed people's attitudes. Corruption started to soar and overshadowed almost every citizen. Almost everyone became active in taking Iran to new depths of moral collapse.

None of these moral failures mattered to the mullahs. Instead they defended their actions with the relevant Quranic and Islamic references, calling their rule "social justice" and "compassion," and labeling others as "Israeli (or American) agents".

Under repression and fear many of our relatives were unconsciously turned into spies for the mullahs. Since the problems of a person in Islam are also counted the problems of his family or community, every family or community was compelled to watch the behaviors of others in order to avoid problems as much as they could. If your parents or community leaders doubted your behavior, they would immediately warn you, or call a religious guard if you ignored their warnings and continued your opposition. Because of fear, friends betrayed friends, handing them over to the mullahs' persecuting guards. Many were imprisoned, tortured, given life-time imprisonment and slaughtered. Others were forced into drug addiction to destroy their zeal for freedom and discourage other youth from supporting opposition.

It had only seemed like yesterday that our dictator king was replaced by a peace-loving mullah, the Ayatollah Khomeini, with a promise of freedom and prosperity. "Our back bones were broken," as Iranians say, and we were left paralyzed in every aspect. We were angry at ourselves for our ignorance and our failure at having a sound vision for the future of our country. The Mullahs' very clever deception impaired our visions and plans, and made us unable to anticipate our future with them.

The mullahs were a minority before the Revolution. We were not aware that they had no option but to wait with patience and guile. They knew that Islamic dominance would not take place with sincerity and openness. They even endured the relatively secularist approach of the interim government in the first year after the Revolution, as secularism is contrary to Islam's harsh political philosophy[7] and waited for the right time to act. They sought for the right moment when hunting their prey: they waited and eventually succeeded. They did

---

7   Q9:123.

not lose their temper even when Dr Banisadr—known as pro-Western by the mullahs, won the presidential election with 80% of people's vote a year after the Revolution. They knew that this was a great victory for pro-democratic Iranians. They knew that they needed time to confuse people and bring their very subtle and tactical maneuver into work in order confuse people and redirect the Revolution from its main purpose. They did so by chasing three crucial tactics patiently.

First, they challenged people and said if they were true Muslims they needed to follow the foot-steps of Muhammad and his so-called rightly-guided successors in order to gain the favor of Allah. Leadership in Islam has an incredible appeal with Muslims who are greatly dependent on Islam and desire to trust their so-called holy leaders in order to reserve a righteous life that secures them from the punishment of Allah in the afterlife. For this, Muslims need to believe in the sovereign rights of those who rule in Muhammad's place: Muhammad and his successors had sovereign rights over people and everything. The Ayatollah Khomeini also needed to establish such a right if Iranians Muslims wanted to live with Islam and for Allah. People called themselves Muslims, but until then they had never been publicly challenged by a leader that they were not living an Islamic life, since they were not following and imitating a religious leader. They were told it was time for them to take their faith in Islam seriously.

With this challenge, the mullahs brainwashed us first and then took the idea to the parliament as a bill, passed it as a law and therefore established a sovereign right for the Ayatollah Khomeini legally as the supreme leader. This crafty approach worked among our fellow Muslims and chained us to the absolute dictatorship of Khomeini and his successors to the end. Now, nobody had any right to challenge his decisions and nothing could be legitimate without his approval. Once I said in a public talk, "Iran will not have freedom if we do not support good ideas and creativity, but criticize static ideas. We need to be able to criticize everything and everybody even our leader, the Ayatollah Khomeini. Because everybody can be wrong or make a mistake." This was used as a reason for my death sentence, since mullahs believed that the Ayatollah Khomeini could never be wrong.

The President Banisadr had met with some of the mullahs and expressed his concern that the absolute right of a leader is the complete loss of freedom. He however was not able to fight against the very identity of Islam in the presence of a majority Muslim, as this would have cost him his life and position. The bill was finally passed and yoked all Iranians to the power of the Ayatollah Khomeini.

The mullahs' second approach was to denigrate the plans of democratic groups and characterize them as non-Islamic agents of the West, since they were using the word "democracy" which was a construct of the West. They succeeded in this also, since the general mind-set was already prepared against the West by the revolutionaries. The mullahs said that Iran did not need a western style democracy but an Islamic style democracy in which people are only free to do what Islam commands. Freedom is for following Muhammad but not for rejecting him.

Their third approach was to put the sovereign right of the Ayatollah Khomeini into practice and deal with opposition according to the Shari'a, the law of Islam. It was after this that any opposition to the mullahs turned into an uphill battle and failure. It was at this point that president Banisadr was attacked by rockets, his presidency collapsed and he had to run for his life.

Of course a fourth component was neeeded for the mullahs to protect them nationally and fulfill their mission internationally. The two branch of Iranian version of Hezbollah, *Sepah* and *Basigis*, were created so that these armies could rescue them from any possible coup, similar to what happened in 1953 AD to the revolutionary Prime minister of Iran, Dr Mosaddegh and the coup returned the Shah to power again. Because of this, the mullahs closely watched the officers of the general army who were trained by the Shah and promoted only those officers who showed loyalty to the mullahs.

The mullahs' second goal in establishing Hezbollah was to invade countries around Iran, destroying the signs of western secularism and preparing Muslim nations to capture Israel. They wanted a Middle-East without Israel and western influence.

In the meantime, the mullahs started to invest huge amounts of the country's wealth in Lebanon and Syria. They wanted to strengthen the Hezbollah to gain power in Lebanon and establish Iran as the number one enemy to Israel in the region. They began to employ everybody who ame to them, especially younger people, to establish a stronger Hezbollah (army of Allah) in Lebanon.

All these elements show that the mullahs were the best organized group, who had a plan to dominate Iran rapidly, even though they were in minority. We were all shocked at how these minority mullahs captured the country in a short time after the Revolution and were able to silence the majority.

A Fourteen Hundred Year Old Problem

We were cleverly deceived so that we could foolishly and blindly surrender ourselves to the mullahs in Iran. In the years before the Revolution, they seemed open-minded so we shared our feelings with them. They were great listeners then, but after the Revolution the same mullahs terrified us and our families. The moral sickness they displayed choked our hearts with fear. They started with terrorizing individuals. Then they massacred communities who favored to local leaders. They slaughtered thousands of our contemporary innocent Kurds, something Iran experienced when Arabs invaded Iran in 7th century AD or when Genghis Khan swept over Iran in 13th century AD.

People like me who have survived death in the Middle-East and taken shelter in the West cry out to western communities to be aware of the radical Muslims' amibitions. However many offer excuses to avoid the issue. Some say that western people have established freedom strongly, so Islamists will not be able to take over. But they say this at a time when Islamists have already strengthened their roots, penetrated many political arenas, established Shari'a in some areas, and are posing a great threat to life in the West. Our own personal testimonies and experiences, that speak volumes about Islamists, are ignored or discounted. Why should we not be at least be a little worried that Islamists in the West may follow the footsteps of their peers who shed the blood of millions in Islamic countries? Sadly, many who are deceived by Islamists do not want to face the truth, but unwisely take the easy option of assuming that Islam will be different in the West. They choose to ignore the words and deeds of Islamists in the West, which point to the fact that Islam cannot be compatible with any democratic values and Islamists will not be able to tolerate democracy after they gain power.

Minority Islamists in Iran approached us in a similar way they are approaching people in non-Islamic societies. None of us who were fighting for freedom could have imagined that our unity with the mullahs would pave the way for their tyrannical rule that rejects justice. That's why we are crying loud and pleading that people should not trust Islamists or anyone else who says that Islam is a religion of peace.

In Iran, we were unable to discover that the fundamental problem was not the committed followers of Islam, but Islam itself. It is Islam that leads mullahs to establish a Bedouin-style rule in Iran. It was Islam that guided the heavy hands of Islamic governments to prevent Iranians from relying on the great values of their culture, which cherished individual rights and pushed back Islam's inhumane values. Cyrus the great king left a great legacy for us to resist fascism. This legacy has never been so raised up in the history of Iran since the invasion of Islamists as it was in the time of Shah. We were proud of our culture and did not believe that Islamists could take over in the face of what we had inherited from the great king Cyrus:

> *I [Cyrus] announce that I will respect the traditions, customs and religions of the nations of my empire and never let any of my governors and subordinates look down on or insult them while I am alive. From now on (...) I will impose my monarchy on no nation. Each is free to accept it, and if any one of them rejects it, I never resolve on war to reign. While I am king of Iran, Babylon, and the nations of four directions, I never let anyone oppress any other, and if it occurs, I will take his or her right back and penalize the oppressor. And while I am monarch, I will never let anyone take possession of movable and landed property of the others by force or without compensation. While I am alive, I prevent unpaid, forced labor. Today, I announce that everyone is free to choose a religion. People are free to live in all regions and take up a job provided that they never violate other's rights. No one should be penalized for his or her relatives' faults. I prevent slavery and my governors and subordinates are obliged to prohibit exchanging men and women as slaves within their own ruling domains...*[8]

Under the creed of Cyrus, a government cannot restrict the rights of people and dominate their rights, beliefs, emotions and everything else. He is saying that as the king of kings, he is ready to limit his rights for the freedom of people.

He left a legacy which encouraged us to stay out of other's lives and let fellow citizens, no matter what their rank, race or religion, put their ideas into practice and exercise their creativity for the good of their country and communities. As a successful king, Cyrus knew that no community could survive

---

8   United Nations Human Rights Council -13th session (1-26 March 2010). Statement by David G. Littman—Wednesday (2:45 pm), 40th plenum, 24 March 2010.

without individual autonomy and achievement. He decided to stand for individuals' freedom.

We never thought that Islamist would be able to rise to power in the face of our Iranian culture and in the face of the 20th century's civilization.

How could the democratic and participative values of this great king, which so shaped our culture, give way to the authoritarian and repressive principles of mullahs, permitting Islam to take over our lives?

Islam is the number one religion for promoting deception. The Quran says that Allah is the best of deceivers.[9] What can be expected from Allah's committed followers if their spiritual leader is known as the best of deceivers? This is what the non-Islamic societies in the world need to know about Iran. They need to understand what Islam does to the citizens of a country if they ignore the internal components of Islamic teachings. We were deceived very subtly.

No matter how long Islamists live with people, and no matter how many times people discover their deceptions, they are still clever in hypnotizing people and deceiving them continually. They seek out new methods of deception in order to yoke people.

Iran has been the battleground between Persian and Arabian cultures from the first day of the Islamist's invasion. Iranians continued to remember Cyrus and Darius the great kings but mullahs schemed to redirect and control their minds. Throughout the Islamic history of Iran, Islamists knew that they could not separate Iranians from their past. Before the Revolution if a person spoke against the kings Cyrus and Darius, he would lose his place in the community. Aware of this nationalistic solidarity, the Islamists had planned a new way to destroy the patriotic behavior of Iranians after the Revolution. They strove to falsely identify themselves with

---

9   Q8:30.

people in order to establish themselves strongly among the people and then destroy them from the inside out. Since the rise of Islam to the Iranian Revolution of 1979, Islamist mullahs had never mixed intimately with Iranian culture. Everybody in Iran knew that they were the representatives of Arabian culture in practice and opposed those who cherished our Persian culture. We were Muslims in the context of our Persian identity. As practicing Muslims, we were sometimes under the impact of mullahs, but felt guilty spiritually for holding our culture above Arabia's culture in the time of the Shah, fearing that Allah would punish us. However the common love for the country was strong and was justified in one way or the other.

Mullahs in Iran were dealing with such people. They always wished Iranians to be like Egyptians, Iraqis, Syrians, Lebanese and others who had lost their national identities and called themselves 'Arabs' because of their trust in Islamists and of their loose attachment to their cultures and languages. But Iranians were different. They had frustrated the Iranian mullahs for centuries with their strong patriotism. At the beginning of 16th century AD, Sheikh Safi-Alddin Ardabili, a radical mullah from northern Iran, established himself with a strong army, captured the whole of Iran, and made Islam the formal religion of Iran, opening the door for Arabian culture. Yet even with his great army he was unable to extinguish the culture of monarchy in Iran, and his descendants had no choice but to establish themselves as kings in order to win the favor of Iranians. As a result, Arabian culture lost another opportunity.

Our contemporary mullahs had to use all their skills of manipulation to destroy the great legacy Iranians inherited from Cyrus and Darius, so they could establish themselves and forever prevent Iranians from challenging them. That was what we experienced from days after the Revolution. With the help of some leftists, mullahs called the 'kingdom' unfashionable. They established the Hezbollah in Iran, a strong military power which aimed to destroy our culture and free values. After this, they attempted to export terrorism through Hezbollah and kill even fugitive pro-monarchists and democratic Iranians abroad. Over the past thirty years they have killed or disabled many Iranians in other countries, especially in the West.

The Ayatollah Khomeini said to Iranians before the Revolution that it would be all right with him if Iranians wanted the monarchy again after the collapse of Shah. He knew that Iranians wouldn't want to separate themselves from the kingdom system and from Iran's founding kings. Before the revolution he was afraid to fight the kingdom culture of Iran directly. We never asked, if he was genuine in his words, why he had never spoken about a possible successor for the Shah. This was the usual case in Iran's kingdom history. Our passive thoughtlessness meant we did not question his focus on overthrowing the Shah and left future plans for the future.

Another reason for Iranians to lose to the mullahs was that the West, especially America under the presidency of Jimmy Carter, withdrew from supporting the Shah, and believed in Khomeini's lies when he said he would establish a democratic country.

The third reason for us to lose to the mullahs was they were better organized than other groups in the country for a complete takeover. We were just a bunch of people (mostly young) who loved democracy without knowing or planning a path to democracy.

The fourth reason for the mullah's success was their commitment to kill or be killed for the restoration of Shari'a and the Islamic imperialism of the caliphate. For them the end justifies the means. They got their way through deception, intimidating and eventually murdering reformers. They even killed some mullahs who were of the same rank and in competition with them. Before the Revolution they joined with the students who fought for democracy. This was a new deceitful tactic that has never been used by Islamists since the rise of Islam. They knew that Islam rejected democracy. But this time they were deceitfully humble, tolerant and flexible with convincing attitudes. They amazed us and entrusted the leadership of the Revolution to them. In reality, they were the more ideological and disciplined revolutionaries, whose ambition was to mask their aims. They showed patience, pretending to be modest in order to gain momentum. Their long-term goal was held secret until they attained power and revealed their ferocious attitudes to us when we were no longer able to compete with their cruelties. Many kept silent, many died and many others fled the country as a result.

The fifth reason for the mullahs' easy take-over was their zeal for war. They are masters in creating tensions and making wars. For Islamists war is always a good tool for restricting the freedom of nationals. They create enemies and start wars. Time after time, the Ayatollah Khomeini announced that the country was at war: war with Iraq, war with Israel, war with the West, and war with the national enemies. In a state of war, nobody has the right to criticize his government and thereby create a pretext for the nation's enemies. The mullahs' goal in all of this was to demonize western democracy and modernity and make their authoritarian caliphate a role model for the future of Iran. They subtly gained the support of some western leaders in the name of democracy, redirected the Revolution and demolished the kingdom of Shah, because they feared that the Shah would open his country to western democracy more and more, while taking people further from Islam. War was a good option for the mullahs to stop the spread of western democracy.

A sixth reason for the mullahs' success to overcome us was their ruthless approach to people. No coherent logic works for them; their logic is belligerent assertion. If you use reason against them, your finger tips and head must be chopped off. Life, laws and relationships are all disregarded in the name of Allah. They were free to break laws for the sake of Allah and invade people's personal lives. They never believed that laws could apply to them. They attained power at the cost of people's freedom and rights. After the Revolution, I experienced time and again their use of threats to extort of money from people (mainly the wealthy) in order to finance their terroristic plans. They were charging families for every bullet used in killing someone from that family who stood in their way.

The mullahs kept all these plans secret and showed themselves to us as moderates before the Revolution. We did not understand the implications of their words and were unable to see beneath the surface of their doctrines, which gave them rights to deceive even their own children if the conditions necessitated. Their artificial kindness controlled our minds so that we were not able to maintain a balanced relationship with them. Their subtle presentations induced us to follow them and pay any price to oust the Shah. We were unable to think about what would happen if they changed their minds in the future and wanted to get involved in politics. These mullahs were well prepared and were able to 'play' us. They used words such as *freedom* and *prosperity* to make us believe that what they intended was not any different from what we intended. Before the Revolution, they never spoke about the Islamization of Iran, only about the liberation of Iran from dictatorship.

Their words and attitudes were so different after taking power. Their real agenda was that they wanted to release Iran from the influence of western democracy and freedom, and rule over it by the principles of Islam. They hated the slightest innovation that reflected the West. For this reason they aspired to kill all those who wanted democracy. They did everything to yoke the country under the rule of Islam and advance their ideology. They spread their radical narrative into every school, university, organization and into mainstream journalism. For the cause of Islam they sacrificed every scholarly standard that would give knowledge of freedom and prosperity to people. They imparted indoctrination on ancient-Arabian nomadic culture. They indoctrinated the university students and ensured that anyone with their own opinion would never get a university degree. The same policy applied to those who wanted jobs. Their repression went to such an extent that many families and communities encouraged at least one of their family members to become a religious guard so that he could play the role of a mediator and rescue them in times of difficulty.

It is always after gaining power that Islamists reveal their true colors and surprise people with intolerance. Contemporary uprisings in Islamic countries and Islamists' access to power have always proven the dualistic nature of Islamists. It is heartbreaking that this deception has been at work in many Islamic countries but no Muslim nations has been able to learn a lesson and discern the crafty nature of Islam. They would rather blame fundamentalist groups for 'hijacking' Islam. After the rise of the Ayatollah Khomeini in Iran, hundreds of unhappy Muslims who protested against the mullahs were killed simply because they believed that the mullahs did not follow true Islam. This is the response we receive from many moderate Muslims who say that Islam is a religion of peace, but Islamists are hijacking it. Unfortunately, moderate Muslims do not know and do not want to know Islam for themselves. They have just been compelled to repeat from childhood that Islam is inherently good, peaceful and nothing bad could exist in it.

Islam has deprived Muslims nations of free thinking and speaking. This Islamic problem enabled the mullahs to redirect the educational principles of our country to reflect Mecca's unquestionable nomadic principles. Because of Islam the mullahs abandoned impartiality, rejected the education of females, and showed hostility to non-Islamic values. They disrespected Iranian history, replacing the thousands of years old logo "lion" on the Iran's national flag with the Arabian logo of "Allah". They robbed the younger generation of knowledge about the history and ideals of their country which their forefathers had passed on from generation to generation. But those young people who did not look Islamic and refused to wear a beard did not have access to jobs and education. Girls who gave weight to the culture of their forefathers were tortured or denied basic rights. Iranians from minority groups were treated as second class citizens and persecuted because of their beliefs.

This is what Islamists have been doing to their people over the last 1400 hundreds years of Islamic history. They stripped them of their national honor and deprived them economically, culturally and morally. They fought creativity and blocked the doors of prosperity to their nations. They prospered only when they occupied and looted other lands, as the Ottoman Empire did. Their political principles only served their own interests for establishing the Islamic Shari'a.

The Islamists' backward law and culture helped neither Iranians nor any other Muslim nations in the world. Islamists never want to see the forest for the trees; they see everything through the eyes of an Arabian dry and lifeless culture. Any time they had an opportunity to rule they created a community in which the atmosphere of hate led to ongoing political and social violence.

Still Aimed to Serve

Although discriminations and hostilities were increasingly shadowing us day after day, we still aimed to do something for the country in any way we could, as long as we were allowed to breathe. We could not imagine that the mullahs could be so deceptive and hostile. We learnt our bitter lessons gradually. A famous mullah even said openly in his television talk that if a mullah is in power no one will be able to bring him down unless he is dead and does not have anyone to continue his mission. He will never let himself to be voted out of office and never allow the government of Allah to fall into the hands of a less faithful person or an infidel.

This is the major reason for the Islamist Republic of Iran to remain in power for more than three decades. The mullahs have used a system that tightly controls people in the Shari'a frame as a means for slaving them to their fundamentalist government. People have no choice but show allegiance to them to survive or prosper.

However, we, the lovers of democracy, were counting on the people's 80% vote which was cast in favor of the president Banisadr in the first presidential election. We thought people would not forget their first zeal easily but keep it for the next parliamentarian election. We also thought that if the mullahs allowed us to nominate a candidate in the future, and we regained a measure of power, people would be encouraged to stand behind us more courageously.

The president's escape discouraged many of us who were his colleagues and had battled hardships with him. How could a people's president escape for the sake of his own life and leave millions of his followers as orphans? Despite all the difficulties I did not want to allow our loneliness to disappoint us in fighting for freedom. I was still hoping to reach parliament in the second election and speak up more strongly, alongside other opposition leaders who remained in the country and remained in the parliament from the first parliamentary election. I was thinking that the mullahs would quickly lose their position among Iranians and would not increase their vote. My hope lay in the dissatisfaction of many Iranians dealing with the economic hardship caused by the mullahs. Many people secretly expressed their dissatisfaction to me.

MUSLIM
KILLS
MUSLIM

8

Arrested!

Prison

The second election for parliament drew closer. I had announced my candidacy, but had to wait for the time of formal enrollment before I could begin campaigning. I believed that the mullahs' repressions had alarmed many exhausted Iranians, causing them look for a way to save their country, which was on a path to unsustainable bankruptcy. I was disappointed and decided to stay away from the Islamic political philosophy this time. I was trying to align my desires with the nation's cultural wisdom and hoped to rise as an Iranian star along with other Iranian zealots, and save the country from the mullahs' tyranny.

Little did I know that the mullahs did not believe in elections and they only allowed an election to find out who their competitors were. Once they identified a rival they did every vicious thing in their power to destroy them and those patriotic Iranians who genuinely loved their country and wanted freedom. The mullahs did everything they could to stop individuals from uniting people under the umbrella of their national culture. What mattered for them were the values of Islam. They not only showed hostility to the Iranian culture, but tried to destroy its power to unify the various communities of the nation.

At this time we started to dig into our country's history and unearthed the politics of the ancient day Arabian Islamists who dominated our country. The motto they spread around was that Islam was perfect and Islamism could give them everything. Because of this the people desired to adopt the religion Islam. The truth was the Arabs invaded Iran but found they could not rule over this developed nation easily. To dominate every aspect of Iranian life they used a similar tactic to what our contemporary mullahs used before the Revolution of 1979. They too had promised prosperity and a peaceful and respectful Islam which later destroyed the peace of the nation and treated the Iranians as second class citizens.

Deep in our hearts, we were so sorry that we had not investigated the Islamists' political philosophy and were not wise enough to see the mullahs' deceits. We trusted their empty words and thought that their values would give us more than the kingdom of the Shah. Their post-revolutionary attitudes caused us to blame ourselves for opposing the Shah under whose kingdom we had a measure of freedom and were able to call ourselves Iranians.

Now, not only did we lose the hope of freedom under the mullahs' dictatorship, we lost the hope to live. Freedom of speech became something imaged which we could only long for under their suppression. Not only this, our families were living in horror. Anytime we heard the bell on our gate ringing, we would think that it could be religious guards come to take us somewhere unknown. Our homely comforts were giving way to increasing fear and horror.

Soon enough it was my turn to be abducted and taken away.

My wife and I and our three-year-old daughter went to visit my in-laws in the city one night. A man with several guards went to my mother's house, saying that he had come from Rasht, the capital city of our state Gilan, and wanted to discuss the upcoming election with me. Unable to speak Persian, my mother called my older brother to speak with the man.

When my brother informed him where I was he asked my brother to take him and his companions to me. My brother drove his own car and they followed him. When they reached the house, my brother was thanked and told that he could go. Two of the men rang the bell and asked for me to go to the gate to speak with Dr Khazaei, who was the Chief Executive Officer of the head office of the branch subsidiary organization, *Building Jihad*, which I led before. Out of respect, my brother-in-law asked them to come in and have a cup of tea with us. They said that Dr Khazaei was sitting in his car parked in the street and wanted to have a short talk with me about my activities for the coming election.

My brother-in-law came and told me, "Two guards are at the gate, saying that Dr Khazaei is parked in his car and wants to speak with you." Dr Khazaei and I respected each other, and he was aware of the mullahs' hatred of me. I went to the gate and asked the guards, "Where is Dr Khazaei? My goodness! Why is he not coming in?" One of them responded, "We are only accompanying him. He is in the car. He does not have much time. Would you please come to the car and have a short chat with him? We have to go as soon as possible."

I went to the car, looked in, and saw the other two guards, but Dr Khazaei was not in the car. I immediately realized I had a problem. I said to the two young guards outside, "Dr Khazaei is not in the car!" They said they were Khazaei's friends and had come to convey a message. They wanted me to get into the car but I refused. As I started to walk away they brought out their guns from under their coats, put them to my head and pushed me into the car.

The thugs covered my head and face with a beanie, handcuffed me, and drove the car through various streets so that I was no longer able to determine our direction. Eventually, I found myself in a horrifying place, the Prison of the Revolutionary Guard in my hometown.

Unaware what the consequence of a complaint would be in a political prison, I complained to them and said, "Did you need to kidnap me at night time? I am not a fugitive. I am always in the city, in the streets and shopping centers. You could have come to me anytime you wanted. Why do you take pleasure in causing pain to my family? Why didn't you want them to know that you guards have brought me here?"

Though I do not like to recall the horrifying moments in prison, these questions plagued me during that painful time. They were also significant after my escape from Iran and subsequent conversion to Christ in Turkey. I read Jesus' comments to the crowd which was sent by Jewish priests and elders to arrest Him. I became overcome with emotion as I recalled my own experience. I discovered that Jesus asked the same question of the multitude upon his arrest in the dark of night.[1] Socially, politically and emotionally, I was able to identify my pains with His pains and was ready to listen to His story. I know now that He allowed these things, though painful, so that one day they would draw my attention to Him.

Torture

I never imagined that a committed Muslim would torture and persecute a fellow Muslim with unimaginable cruelty. People had told me before but I did not believe that the mullahs' persecution and torture could be so severe until I experienced it personally. The things I saw were unthinkable in their brutality. No one, except those who have experienced the bitterness of political prison in the Islamic Republic of Iran can possibly understand the treachery of such a prison. Years later in America I met three Iranians in a restaurant randomly. During our conversation they learned in which prison I had been incarcerated. One of them, whose husband had been in the same prison, began to weep. She told us what had happened to her husband. Many prisoners desire to die as soon as possible in order to be freed from that persecution

---

1   Matthew 26:47, 55-56.

but instead they are humiliated and terrorized time and time again. One prisoner used his pajamas to hang himself from the iron frame of a little window in his cell but the material was so old it was not strong enough to hold his weight and suffocate him. The man wept, wanting to release himself from unbearable pain, and cursed his pajamas.

On the night that I was kidnapped, I was wearing my pajamas. One of my captors was beating my face and saying, "You wanted to rescue a nation from mullahs, but now rescue yourself and let us see it." While mocking me, they were pulling at my pajamas and asking me, "Who is going to sleep with your wife tonight?" Another said, "Who can sleep with her, as he is going to die? She is yours or mine, he will not be around anymore, he is going to die."

For three days, I endured emotional and physical shock and pain. Emotional because it was unbelievable to hear and see such immoral words and attitudes from the Muslims who had introduced themselves to people as righteous and compassionate.

In the hours when I wasn't being tortured, I was taken to a cell that was really a hole in the ground used as a toilet. The first month in the prison is vital to the persecutors, forcing prisoners to confess the things they want to hear. Whenever they wanted to get rid of someone they forced other prisoners to falsely testify against him. One day, a young man and I were taken to the torture room. He was slashed with cable to make him falsely testify that I financially supported the Mojahedin-e Khalgh, a faction which opposed the Islamic Republic of Iran. Three times they slashed him to the point of fainting but each time he refused to lie against me. They became so angry and started to cut one of his ears off. Unable to bear the pain, the young man finally testified against me. His torturers left his ear on.

Judged

After two months my wife learned my whereabouts. The revolutionary judge in our area, who was also a mullah, lied to her. He told her I had killed innocent people and must face justice. She was told to forget me and that I had not been a faithful Muslim husband for her. They encouraged her to express her anger toward my deceit when she was allowed to see me. "Very soon we will bring him to a television show, and you will hear from his own mouth what horrifying things he has done," the judge told her. He also said to her, "We will look after you if you like." What the judge really meant was, "Divorce him and be mine or one among those who follow the Ayatollah Khomeini."

My wife, discouraged, received permission to visit me. Through tears she asked me, "Why did you hide all the terrible things you have done?" She repeated to me the things she had heard from the judge. The mullahs were poisoning the minds of my wife and our community. I told her, "They are lying. They are trying to discourage you, separate you from me and torture me emotionally. They are also trying to get rid of me. That's why they are trying to confuse my family and the community with their lies. I have not killed anyone. I am not a killer; it is they who are killers. I haven't done anything wrong. I am here only because of my opposition to them. Please let everyone know this as much as you can."

My words gave my wife courage and she spread my message throughout the community.

I was taken to court for the first hearing. The court for political opposition is called the Revolutionary Court. Judgment of political prisoners takes place in a closed room with only a few religious guards, the judge, and the prisoner present. My judge was an ignorant mullah who not only did not deserve the position but also did not know how to judge. Injustice is at the root of every Islamic revolutionary Judge. The revolutionary judges are placed in such a position not because of their capabilities but because of their allegiance to top leaders. According to the Islamic Republic of Iran, they should not be merciful towards opponents; they are only to inflict pain on anyone who criticizes the system.

It was embarrassing and painful for me to be judged by such a man. "Why don't you join the Friday Prayer, like many other prisoners do?" The judge's first question was meant to stump me, but I was not afraid to respond boldly as I realized him to be unaware of Islamic teachings concerning this. "As I understand, sir, if you do not trust an imam, you do not stand imitating him in prayer. I do not trust the Friday Imam. And I do not believe that Allah will ignore my prayers in prison," I responded.

It is a custom in Islam that on Fridays, many committed Muslims go to a mosque and pray under the leadership of a Friday Imam (a mullah who is called *Imam Jum'a*). In order to fulfill their religious duties or to gain the favor of the revolutionary guards, some prisoners enlisted to join the Friday Prayer in our town. They were taken to a mosque under a tight security program and placed in the prisoners' spot for prayer. I did not join the Friday prayers. To my astonishment, the guards had reported this to the judge. This is a very personal decision; judges do not discuss this in the court. It damages their own prestige if they include such a personal issue in a court case. My judge included it, because he was not a real judge; he was a persecutor.

However, after he heard my bold response, he looked unhappy and said to me, "I do not believe that your only problem is the Friday Imam. You do not accept any of us. Do you believe that we represent justice?"

I responded, "You cannot represent justice, sir."

I continued, "Have you ever studied justice? Justice says, 'Do not lie,' but you lied to my wife. Justice does not oppress the innocents, but you are keeping an innocent man in your prison simply because he does not agree with everything you do. How can I call you a just judge, sir?"

"It seems to me that you are certain you are going to die. Therefore, you feel free to say whatever you like," said the judge.

I replied, "Yes sir, I am ready to die. You are in the prison of your own world and will not be able to listen to me. I have to say what I believe. You want me to keep quiet, but I cannot. I am the leader of thousands. How can I betray them? And you really don't need to ask questions of your prisoners to determine whether or not you are an agent of death. Since you were appointed to this position, many people have come to realize that communities have been put under the shadow of death. People are not dumb. These people have a history of many dictators, none of whom were able to survive."

One of the guards asked permission to beat me, but the judge waved him off, saying, "He is already dead to me, son. He is just breathing his last moments. You won't have to beat him again. Your torturing brothers at the prison will find a solution for his tongue."

Back to "University"

The judge turned to the guards, "Take him to the university (prison)." The guards blindfolded me and took me to their university of pain and torture.

The mullahs have no respect for universities, but education is revered by Iranians. Education is a legacy their forefathers left for them. Centuries ago, people from many nations came to study in the former Persia. Sadly, the more the Arabian nomadic and Islamic culture captured the minds of Iranians, the more they backslid in education. However, the Ayatollah Khomeini called his prisons 'universities' in jest, knowing they would be used to rape and torture women and men who opposed them, and these would **teach** lessons to many Iranians to avoid rejecting his regime. Young opposition boys were and continue to be slaughtered or forcibly addicted to drugs so they would lose strength and be unable to fight the mullahs.

The previous prisoners, who were kept in the same toilet where I was, wrote on the wall, "This toilet is called a university by the Ayatollah Khomeini and the Islamic Republic of Iran. This is a place that made our children orphans or made our parents and families mourn forever. We were not able to see one good thing and learn one good lesson in this university. Oh, Iran! What turned your universities into toilets and prisons? Isn't it because you are closing your eyes to the unjust mullahs? There is a vast difference between this university and universities where students are taught to be a blessing to their nation and uphold freedom."

The news of my fearless response to the judge was spread throughout the city. The source was the angry guards, who relayed my fearless insolence toward the judge. Some admired my courage. The news reached my wife, who knew the penalty for such opposition. She began to lose hope for my release.

A Three Year Old Visitor

My little daughter missed me and cried for me to come home. My wife went to the judge and asked him to allow a visit for my daughter. She asked for the meeting to be in a court office instead of the horrifying environment of the prison.

I missed my daughter very much but did not want the environment of the prison to be etched in her mind forever. Also, I did not want my captors to see any emotional weakness (which is power for me) on my part. If she visited I would show love and cry to my daughter. They would use my parental love to cause me more suffering. One of the tactics they used was to bring prisoners' children in and threaten to harm them in order to break the prisoners' spirits.

After many requests, my wife was granted permission to bring my daughter for a visit in the court building. I was blindfolded and handcuffed for the drive. The driver, to my surprise, treated me with respect and took the blindfold from my eyes but left me cuffed. Inside the court gate, I raised my head and saw my daughter playing on the steps of the court building. With a heart-melting sigh, unique to my culture, I raised my voice saying, "Oh, may I die for you my darling." Impulsively, I opened the door while the car was still running. For a moment, I forgot that I was a prisoner and needed permission to exit the car. All I could think of was to throw my arms around my daughter.

When I opened the door, the driver braked suddenly to prevent an accident. I was crying, apologizing. My uncontrollable behavior to see my child impacted the guard to the point of tears. Quietly he said, "It's okay. You can get out." I ran toward my daughter, and when she saw me, she cried and I cried. She asked me, "Where were you? Why didn't you take me with you?" We went into the building, where precious time passed quickly. The moment of separation was hard. Would we see each other again? I tried to comfort my daughter, telling her how much I loved her and making a promise to see her again—a promise I wasn't sure I could keep. That moment was more painful to me than when I had been kidnapped. Before, I was unsure what would happen to me. Now, I sensed the smell of death.

New Living Quarters

The day after my visit, I was called from my cell and told to make myself ready. *Ready for what? To be taken somewhere else? To go home? Or to die?* The uncertainty was like a death sentence. Despite expecting the savage mullahs to do every evil thing, I was still crying in my heart to the supernatural One to release me from their further horrific plans, persecutions, and prisons.

Later, a religious guard came and gave me a blindfold to cover my eyes. He took my hand, led me through a door, and took the blindfold off and I found myself in a room with six prisoners. A few of us recognized one another, but even those I was not familiar with recognized me from my campaign as a political candidate. As soon as they saw me, they stood up in respect. Those closest to me rushed forward and hugged me, crying. We had an hour, a time of emotion and laughter. I asked them how long they had been there. A few were brought that same day; others had been there longer.

"Do you know why we are here in this room?" I asked them. They were not sure. A few hoped for release. "Sometimes prisoners are brought to a bigger room first," said one of my fellow inmates, "and after the marks of torture disappear from their bodies, they are released. They do not show such a favor to political prisoners unless their prison term comes to an end." To be in a bigger prison room with a few others was a big thing.

The room definitely was not the little toilet where I was kept for three months. We each had a blanket, though we slept on the concrete floor, and we had each other's companionship. Little did we know that the arrangement was a trap. We were together for a month but soon discovered that one of the prisoners was a guard sent to spy on us. Two of the prisoners were taken out and severely slashed by a cable eighty times. They were unable to walk for weeks; we cared for them, and needed to take them to the rest room. Our spy disappeared.

Sometimes a few religious guards came into the cell and showed some respect toward me. Possibly, they were not sure if I would be released. If released I would still be the leader of thousands. Moreover if I was released and I became a leader in the future, I wouldn't be able to ignore their hostility. I believed that some genuinely respected me. They knew that I was innocent and a leader of the people. A few of them brought me food and expressed their sadness with tears.

One day the head of the guards came with a smile, telling me to prepare myself for departure for the following day. The man had been one of my followers, but after I fell out of favor with the mullahs and lost power, he joined the mullahs' party, eventually becoming the head of persecutors in this political prison. I was apprehensive about his smile. The other prisoners were absolutely certain I would be released and go home. Their confidence gave me confidence too. Each of them gave me messages to take to their families. "Enjoy your life," they said; "Remember us when you see the beautiful mountains,. Comfort our families with your words if you are able to visit them." In response, I said to them; "I will never forget you. I will help your families. I will also try my best to find a way and send food to you."

Sentenced!

On the day of my departure we exchanged emotional goodbyes. A mixture of happiness, sadness and fear gripped me. The chief guard led me out without my eyes covered. Because he did not ask me to cover my eyes, I felt more confident that I would be going home. He took me to his room and said that the supreme judge of the state has issued a death sentence for me. I would be moved to another prison in a different state to await my execution. The words hit me hard and my eyes went blur for a moment. Unable to stand on my feet, I leaned against the wall and slid to the floor.

I said to the chief in a barely audible voice, "I am sorry for sitting." He helped me to a chair and called the guards. I was taken to the back of a truck made for carrying prisoners. One of the higher ranking guards handcuffed and blindfolded me. We drove for a few minutes, and the truck stopped. The driver came to the back and asked the guard, who had a gun in his hand, to release my handcuffs and take the blindfold off my eyes. The guard obliged the driver.

"Thank you very much," I said.

"Forgive us for our cruelty," said the driver in response to my surprise. He jumped back into the truck and drove off. My guard looked sad. Both men were younger than I. I was 29. The car headed south of my hometown, down a road where I had walked for 12 years between our house and school; the road I had driven for many years before my political problem and prison. I felt powerless. Tears were frozen in my eyes; I was unable to cry. I wanted to see my family, just for a moment, and then die.

Like a man who is allowed his last request, I asked the guard for a favor, "Would you be able to take me to see my family for a few minutes to say good-bye and leave my clothes at home? They are just a few minutes from here."

He was speechless for a moment. His eyes looked at me so meaningfully. He slowly lifted his head first, brought it down, and closed his eyes. A heavy sigh emerged from his lungs, and he said, "Ah, I wish I was not here and did not have this uniform on."

Then I saw him crying; tears were streaming down his face. I stared at him in amazement. With a compassionate voice he said, "It is your right to see your family and to be with them. More than anybody else, I believe you deserve it. But this is not the right moment. What will happen when your family learns that you are going to die? Won't they mourn and raise their voices and draw the attention of all neighbors? If the mullahs hear this, won't they kill us and you on the spot? Won't they give your family a hard time?"

His argument sounded very wise and I felt embarrassed for such a request. "You are right, brother," I agreed. "I lost control of myself," I said.

Astonished, he said, "You are calling us your brother! We do not deserve to be called your brothers. Brothers solve their problems with each other through words not through guns. We have based everything in our lives on guns, which are ultimately going to kill us too."

His words and company lifted me a bit, and I was able to think. I felt proud of him and thanked him, saying, "You have eased my pain."

I was taken to a revolutionary garrison that also had a prison for those who opposed the mullahs. It was in Rasht, the capital city of our own state Gilan. It was evening, and I was kept there for about an hour. Then a couple of guards came. Once more I was blindfolded and my hands were chained. I was put in the front seat of another car. Someone else was sitting beside me in the front seat in addition to the driver. I didn't know who were in the back seats of the car but from time to time someone coughed from behind me. Immediately I assumed that the rear seats were full.

Apprehension and uncertainty overwhelmed me. The car was hot, and the driver was reckless. I felt sick. I told the driver, "I don't want to create an uncomfortable situation in the car. Could you stop please so that I can get out and have a bit of fresh air?"

The driver did not believe me. He asked, "Are you really feeling sick or are you planning to escape?"

However, he did stop, giving me a respite before resuming the drive. Around midnight, we reached another prison in Chalous, a city in the state of Mazandaran. My captors released me to another team of jailors. I was taken to a room, where four other prisoners were being held. Two of them had been with me only a couple of days before, and asked me to visit their families when I was released. The third man was the one whose ear was almost cut off because of me. When he saw me he came forward, cried, and apologized to me. He said that, while he was being judged, he wrote a letter falsifying his testimony against me, and gave it to the revolutionary judge.

The fourth person in the room was my dear friend, whom I loved but had not seen for years. I had heard that he had been killed in a clash with the mullahs' forces, but that was not certain. For years, he had hidden himself from the mullahs.

He was a militia member of the Mujahidin'e Khalgh of Iran and fought for the Mujahidin until he was eventually caught. Our friendship was not because of politics. His family lived in a village a few kilometers from us towards the Caspian Sea. We attended the same school. While I was a senior high school student, he was in middle school. We saw each other every day. When I was in university and he still in high school, he learned of my financial distress and went to work in a low-paying job in order to help me. I was humbled and grateful but expressed my concern in a thank you note that the extra work could interfere with his studies.

In response he wrote, "In our town, everyone is speaking about your courage and the hardship you went through [to remain in school]. I have two reasons to support you. First, if you fail, I will fail too. Because many fathers, including my father, will be disappointed and eventually will put pressure on their sons to stop their education. Second, I see you as my older brother. I will work in order to help you. When you finish your education and get a job, then you can help me to go through university."

For this reason, I loved him for his thoughtfulness and caring heart. He was a great thinker. He was my friend, and like my little brother, and now I saw that he was going to die with me. We embraced and quietly cried. Had they known we were friends, the guards of this prison would not have put us together for fear of conspiracy against them.

It was hard for me to see my friend carrying a death sentence on his shoulders. I was supposed to get a job and help him finish university. But now the only job remaining for both of us was death; to take our desires with us to the tomb, and leave the ongoing dictatorship of Iran to live longer. The thought of his death reduced the pressure of my death sentence on me. This is the culture of brotherhood in Iran. The pain of the death sentence of the older brother is swallowed up in the pain of his younger brother. I hoped to be taken to the death square ahead of him to spare me the pain of seeing him die.

In the meantime, we were waiting to be separated from each other, so we talked for as long as we could.

The following day, I was taken to another room where four other political prisoners also awaited execution in death row. The rooms had no windows, but there was a small hole in the wall near the ceiling. I could distinguish the sound of the prisoners' slippers from the solid walk of the guards.

For two months, no one was taken from our room to the death chamber. Twice guards came to videotape "confessions" of favor toward the mullahs. My cell mates relented and "confessed", but I refused. They rationalized, saying, "If you speak evil about yourselves and nice about the ruling mullahs, they might reduce your death sentence to life imprisonment." They convinced nearly all prisoners to comply, but those who had death sentences were still killed.

Another Visitor

One day a guard came to our room, telling me to get ready because a high-ranking member of the Revolutionary Guard was coming to speak with me. Confused, I asked, "Do you mean to take the prison pajamas off and put my normal clothes on?"

"No, no, no," he said. "When he comes, you need to stand and do not interrupt him." Then he left. None of us understood why someone of position was coming to see me. I thought it might be another one of their tricks. I was afraid and nervous. Sometimes I wished to die soon and be released from the emotional torture of wondering when it would happen. But what could we do? Nothing.

After an hour, or so, a tall young man in guard's uniform came in. We all stood up. He ordered us to sit and be comfortable.

"Who is Mr Shayesteh?" he asked.

"That's me, sir," I responded.

"How are you?" he asked.

"I am waiting on death row, sir, and it is not a good feeling at all," I said.

"What do you think about Abolhassan Banisadr and where he is now?" the man asked.

Dr Banisadr, the first Islamic president after the Revolution was now in exile, and we were political colleagues.

In response to his questions I said, "I feel good about him. I know that he is an intellectual man and wants to serve his countrymen. The only thing that I do not like about him is that he was not brave enough to stay in his country."

"Do you know that he is a Gharb Zadeh (someone who loves western values at the cost of his own)?" he questioned.

"No," I answered. "I do not know this."

He said, "Yes, he is. We have tried to kill him many times. But because he is protected by the French police, we have been unsuccessful."

I said nothing. This is the attitude of committed Muslims; they call a person Gharb Zadeh if he or she shows favor even to one value of the West.

After a pause, he said to me, "Anyway, I've come here from Tehran to take you to your home today. Take your clothes and be ready to follow me."

For a revolutionary Muslim guard, the "home" of a political opposition was hell. So, to me, his words meant that I was going to be killed that day. I gathered my clothes and, looking at the other four prisoners, said, "*Khoda hafez,*" which means "May God protect you" or "Goodbye" in English.

The guard did not ask me to cover my eyes. He opened the door, went out, and I followed him. He took me to a room, told me to sit, and asked, "What bothered you most these past months in prison?"

"It was most painful to think that I would die unjustly." I said.

He then phoned the revolutionary judge in our town and spoke to him harshly, accusing him of being cruel to me.

So many mind games had been played; I assumed this was another. I learned not to believe anything the guards said. I was right. After his phone conversation, he ordered me to a small cell with no light, saying I would have to wait a few hours before going home. I said to myself, "If he wants to take me to my family home, why didn't he just let me wait in that office instead of this horrible cell?"

After a few hours, another guard came and told me to take off the prison pajamas, put on my own clothes and follow him. He took me back to the same high-ranking guard. He said, "We are going to send you to the prison you have come from. Then we will release you from there."

I said, "If you really want to release me, why are you handing me over to those who destroyed my life, when you have authority to release me from here?"

He said, "Look, we need to help you legally. We know what we are doing. You do not need to worry about this. Go and God bless you."

He ordered the guard who took me from the last cell to take me to my hometown. Within a few hours, I was back in my hometown.

On the way back home, I kept thinking, "Maybe the revolutionary guards are trying to manipulate me as they have done to other political prisoners. Maybe they have realized that many people believe in my innocence and have decided to release me so they can kill me in secret and even mourn with people over my dead body, thinking it would persuade others to believe they had not killed me." My mind raced, scenarios playing like a movie. A death like this was more terrifying to me than death in prison, because it could happen in front of my family and would terrify them. We had seen and heard horrible things from the mullahs in Iran. They are experts in inflicting pain to their opposition, and it is a religious joy for them to torture their oppositions as much as they can.

The driver took me to the prison and handed me over to the same chief who informed me of my death sentence. He opened my documents, looked for a moment and then said, "You are back again!"

He called one of his guards and asked him to take me to a room. It was the guard who was sitting with me on the back of the truck on the way to the second prison, the same guard who wept over my death sentence. He was astonished that I was back. Outside the chief's office, he whispered, "Oh my God, you are back. What is happening brother Shayesteh?"

"I am not really sure what is going to happen," I responded very quietly. I told him what had taken place and how I came to return to this prison. His face was full of excitement. He opened the door to a bigger room, where 13 prisoners sat, mostly young teenagers who were the members of the Mujahidin-e-Khalgh. They rushed forward and said, "Mr Shayesteh, why did they catch you again? And what is this color on your face?" They did not know that I was not released but instead being taken to another prison. I explained how I had been brought back, and then asked, "What is wrong with my face?" I had not seen my face for months because we did not have a mirror. They said it looked as though I had lost much weight and my face was yellowish. I explained that in Chalous, I was in a room with little light. This and the fear of death, I suppose, had drained my face of blood.

I was warned to be careful of what I said in the room; there would be spies disguised as prisoners. The area judge and the prison chief were not happy at all that I was back, and they would do every kind of evil in order to trap me again. I learned that a very young prisoner, who treated me with respect, was a spy. Apparently he showed more respect towards me than to the other prisoners, trying to convince me that he was trustworthy. He was convincing as a prisoner, describing how severely he was persecuted and tortured because of his pro-democracy stand.

Once he cried and said to me, "What do we need to do? Do we keep quiet and die in prison? Don't we need to send this message to people outside and ask them to do something?"

Trying to avoid answering his question, I replied, "I need to listen to you more and hear the words of your heart." In the meantime, I warned the other prisoners that they were to listen to him but not to answer his questions. I suspected that he may have a recording device. I wanted other witnesses against him in case I faced another trial.

One day, the chief guard came into the room with a few other guards to check the room. This boy asked him whether or not he would be permitted to use the rest room. The chief guard allowed him and one of the guards took him to the rest room. After he was brought back he immediately came and sat beside me. I was sitting in a corner alone. He said, "We need to do something. You are a great leader. Why are you keeping quiet? We need your guidance against this cruel government."

I responded, "Do you really respect and accept my leadership?"

"Of course, I do," he said. "I am ready to die for you."

I slapped his face hard, calling him a liar. He rushed to the door, crying for help. "I've been attacked."

A guard opened the door immediately and he rushed out, saying that he wanted to see the chief guard. The chief guard entered the room moments later with more guards. He asked if I had beaten the boy with intent to kill him.

I said, "I did not want to kill him. I just wanted to slap him."

"You know that this will cost you a lot," he said.

"I knew that it would cost me," I said, "but I did this in order to prevent the huge burden he has been trying to load on our shoulders. Time and time again, he encouraged prisoners to plan riots and send messages to the people outside to encourage them to riot against the government. We listened to him each time and did not respond. But today, his deception increased, trying to provoke a response by saying he was ready to die if I told him to die. I hit him for two reasons. First, we will not get involved in his plan to riot against the government. Second, I just wanted to test him in order to see whether he was really honest in saying that he valued me as a leader and was ready to die for me. Every prisoner here knows that he has consistently lied to us."

When I finished, the other prisoners confirmed what I had said and asked for the removal of the traitor. Then the chief guard took me out by the door to talk to me privately. He said, "You ought not to beat a prisoner, no matter what he does. You have to call a guard and report to him."

"I know that I have acted illegally," I said. "I am ready to pay the cost, and I believe my cost is far less than the cost he aims to cause for the country. All the prisoners know that he is a betrayer of our country, and he must face justice." The chief realized that he and his spies had not outwitted the prisoners. He left the room and we never saw the young man again.

I wondered, "What is happening to me? I was told in Chalous that I was going home, but I am still locked up." My temporary release paper was ready, but still unsigned. The revolutionary judge of the area did not want me to be released. But eventually a new judge was appointed and signed the paper, and I was released—temporarily. I was told my documents and death sentence were being reviewed. I had to appear in the revolutionary court the first day (Saturday, in Iran) of each week to show that I was in the city. I could go nowhere without the court's permission.

I even doubted the "review" as being real or just another scheme. Though it was good to be with my family, the fear that at any moment I could be secretly slaughtered by unknown invaders in the night was terrifying.

Family members and many friends were so excited at having me back home from such an ordeal. For days people from many areas came to visit me and expressed their happiness and good will. However, to some of my closest friends, family members and my wife I bluntly told them that this could be a scheme. They were greatly discouraged. I told them that the nature of my release seemed to me strange and it might result in my death in a very mysterious way. I cautioned them to avoid speaking about this in public. The knowledge of my impending death was ever present without verbalizing it, but fear and concern were written on the faces of those who knew this.

Our daughter was growing up and starting to understand things better. "You should not leave me and my mother alone anymore and go again for such a long trip," she would tell me. With sighs, I would respond, "Ah, my beautiful daughter, I am sorry to leave you alone. I do not want to have a journey like that anymore, and I am asking God to keep me near to you always so that together we can destroy loneliness." I could see the uncertainty in my little child in the first weeks after my release while she was playing with her toys or friends. She was so uncomfortable any time I wished to go out. She wanted to make sure that I was not going to break my promise to her. The fear and anxiety in my family caused me to wish many times that I was not a Muslim, did not get involved in the Revolution and politics, so that my family would not have had to bear such pain. But it was too late; the peaceful life was like a hallucination. The more I got caught up in my thoughts, the more I lost hope for my life. Mind-bothering uncertainties and fear were pushing me into the depths of despair. Fear in the Islamic Republic of Iran was multidimensional and a source of torment in every aspect of our lives; fear of joblessness, hunger, humiliation, limitless invasions, etc.

My wife had been working in the mayor's office. She lost her job. The mayor was extremely pro-mullah and hated me. My wife's fear of the mullahs increased when she lost her job because she was my wife. Many family members lost their jobs because their relatives opposed the mullahs. Inflicting hardship and suffering on family members was a tactic the mullahs used to coerce betrayal. If the mullahs made life unbearable for their oppositions' families, because of fear, the families would turn over their children, brothers, sisters, fathers, or mothers to be killed by the butchers working for the mullahs.

9

Midnight Visitors

The door-bell woke us at midnight. We were terrified; thinking my time to die had come. I told my wife, "Be calm. We need to let this go smoothly. If our daughter Narjes wakes up, she will be terrified. You need to take care of her and teach her the honor of our country as long as you are able to live." I said good-bye, assuming it would be my last, and went outside to avoid the guard's entrance into my home to kill me in front of my family.

The fear had already taken away half of my strength. While walking in the front yard towards the gate I dragged my feet on the ground to let them know that they were not ignored. When I opened the gate, I expected guns to be drawn and pointed at my head. I saw two men in revolutionary army uniforms, carrying pistols, standing there without touching their guns. I was speechless. They also didn't speak for a few seconds. Maybe they wanted to make sure that it was me. However, they then began talking quietly, "Please do not be afraid. We are your friends R and A. We had no choice but to come late at night. We do not want anyone to see us or know we are with you."

I was shocked, still unable to speak. I saw that indeed they were my precious old friends who had previously helped me in a crisis. For their safety I am unable to reveal the details of the crisis. I had not seen them for several years due to my separation from the Islamic Republican Party, which they continued to serve. Now my friends had come from far away and were standing before me in the middle of the night. It was like a horrifying dream and my heart grieved to think that it would be these two who would kill me. Mullahs know from the instructions of their prophet that if they persuade someone to kill his friend, the murder will take place quietly.[1]

I learned not to trust anyone I saw in the uniform of the revolutionary army because of my experience in the political prisons. Those who were once our friends were now torturing us as prison guards. To see my friends in this uniform in the middle of the night was terrifying to me. I did not invite them in since I had put in my mind that they had come to kill me. "If this is the case, then let them kill me at the gate rather than inside the house, terrifying my wife and daughter," I said to myself. With a very quiet voice I asked, "Why you? Friends must die for friends according to our culture, but not kill their friends." They looked to each other and then one said, "Are you going to let us in or not? We are still your friends. We cannot talk to you at the gate."

I respected them so much for what they had done for me in the time of the Shah. I said to myself, "Since they are insisting to come in, I should not allow the fear of my death to prevent my respect for them. I should get them in and let my wife and daughter know that I was still appreciative of the sacrifices these two men did to me and even my death could not reduce my love and respect for them". I let them in and closed the

---

1   The Hadith says that Muhammad sent a few of his companion at night to kill one of his critics, a poet named Ka'b bin Al-Ashraf , who also was a famous and generous man. The men who volunteered for the assassination used dishonesty by Muhammad's permission to gain Ka'b's trust, pretending that they had turned against Muhammad and wanted to continue friendship with him. This lie drew the victim out of his house and Muhammad's friends killed him and brought his head for Muhammad (*Bukhari* :: Volume 5 :: Book 59 :: Hadith 369).

gate. I asked them, "Would you please wait here for a moment so I can tell my wife that you are friends? Otherwise she will be scared when she sees your uniforms."

I raised my voice and called to my wife, "I'm okay. Don't be afraid. Two of my old friends have come a long way. They are coming in. We need to look after them."

I asked my friends to sit a while, offering them food and drink. In the meantime my wife joined us. "We do not have time to stay," they said. "We need to leave your house as soon as possible and go back the same way we have come. We will not be able to see each other again. We need to explain now."

As I sat, one of my friends told me of a plan that answered the questions that had been plaguing me since my release. "We have put our lives at risk to release you temporarily. Our legal excuse is that your document must be reviewed. But we are certain that you will not be able to avoid this death sentence unless you escape from the country. The mullahs were clever enough to convince the judge to issue your death sentence. The judge is also an Ayatollah, and the supreme judge would not risk rejecting the death order of an Ayatollah."

I didn't want to escape. The president had escaped and many of his followers and colleagues, including myself, had criticized him for being a coward. I said, "Look! I prefer to die in Iran than to escape."

They appealed to my wife, "You need to encourage your husband to leave the country. If he doesn't leave, he is putting you, your daughter, and us in jeopardy." This matter-of-fact pronouncement preceded my friends' exit.

Escape!

I weighed my options. My enemies were strong. Nothing would stop them from carrying out my death sentence. My friends, realizing my certain demise, used their position, at great risk to themselves and their families, to provide me with

Daniel spending time with his wife and daughter before his escape

a way of escape. Also, if I remained, I would not be allowed to work; critics of the Islamic Republic of Iran had no right to an income. At this time my wife was able to work but was going through a lot of pressure due to her connection with me. Her employment wasn't secure. Even with my wife's meager income my family would live in poverty. Our daughter's education would be jeopardized.

The solution, though painful, was clear. I had to flee Iran. So early in 1985, a few months after the midnight visit, with the help of a few reliable people who worked on the border of Iran and Turkey, I began a journey that would change my life forever.

My name was blacklisted at border control, as was the case with all political opponents whose court cases were yet unfinished.

If your name was in the blacklist you were not permitted to cross the border. I was advised to have my legal passport in hand. This was the passport that I had obtained when I was still in power, before my imprisonment, and it was not expired yet. Those who were helping me cross the border said that a valid passport could save my life if the plan did not work.

We arrived at border control. I was introduced to a customs official who worked at the border where I would gain entry to Turkey. Two other men were in the line to help me get through customs. Their role was to exchange their places with me in the line, if necessary, so that I could pass by the desired customs agent. We did not acknowledge one another to avoid suspicion. Religious guards were everywhere.

As we approached the front of the line, unexpectedly, a guard came forward and started to direct people to two lines. I had been told that the customs agent I had met would call for the next in line. Fear gripped my being: What is going to happen now? Will I make it or not? Will I be sent to the correct line? Or will this be another disaster in my life?

I was between my two helpers but unable to talk to them because the guard was standing close beside us. Under my breath I said, "I don't know what to do." I wasn't sure either man heard me. Should I get out of the line and withdraw from the plan? If I did this what would the other two men do? If we left together the guards probably would stop us and discover our plan. But if I stayed in line, even if I was not able to make it, only I would be caught. The other two would not be charged for conspiracy.

I stayed in the line, surrendering myself to random chance. But I was directed to the other customs agent. When he checked my name in the computer he saw that my name was on the black list and I was not allowed to cross the border. He turned me over to the guards who took me to the office of the chief guard.

"Where are you going?" he asked.

"To Turkey for a few days' holiday, sir," I replied.

"How can you leave with your name on the black list?"

"I was not aware of it, sir."

He ordered one of the guards to take my bag to the room and list the contents in it. He took my passport and gave it to a guard in an adjoining room, ordered him to do something, then came back to his chair. I was standing in the room and the other guard was still there apparently watching me. After ten minutes or so the guard from the other room brought back my passport to the chief with a typed letter.

A Detour

"Your passport is confiscated," the chief said. "We have faxed this letter to the revolutionary judge in your city. You have to take the copy of this letter to the revolutionary judge in your town and inform them what happened. Make sure that you do what you have been told. Otherwise, you invite trouble for yourself and your family."

"Certainly, sir," I responded.

After a few minutes, the other guard came in with my handbag and gave him a sheet of paper with the list of my belongings on it. The chief ordered him to return the bag to me and dismissed me. I left the room and eventually the border control, and walked towards the center of the border town called Makoo to find transportation back to my home.

It was early evening. I did not know what happened to the two men in line who were to help me. All I knew was that one of them was sent through customs before me.

I caught a bus headed to Tehran. I would go there first and head north to Gilan. I was given a window seat at the back of the bus in the row before the last on the left side. The bus drove and a bit later stopped to pick up another passenger. It was a teenager (around 18 or 19 years old) who was led to the aisle seat beside me. Just after sitting, he stretched out his hand to shake mine. Though I thought it strange, I shook his hand. Why would he want a hand shake if we did not know each other? In a situation like this, people only greet each other without a hand shake. A teenager, especially a strange one, never stretches hand to shake the hand of someone older than him, unless the older one stretches his hand first.

"How are you sir?" he asked then.

"I'm OK, thank you."

A few minutes later, I remembered that I had not checked to see if my money was still in my handbag after the guard returned it to me. I opened the bag, pretending to take something, and saw the money but was unable to count it. The boy beside me could be dangerous. The area was infamous as a place unsafe for passengers. In the daytime, the government controlled the area. At night, Kurdish freedom fighters were the authority in many parts. So, the security of the people was not an issue for either faction; it was a thief's haven.

The boy then asked me, "Weren't you let out of the country?"

Frightened, I wondered how he knew of my situation. Perhaps he'd seen me at the border or was one of the guards, now in normal clothes, or was a friend with a guard for a plot. I felt that I was in danger. I countered with a question, "Are we friends that you would try to know about my personal life? Could you please mind your own business?"

He did not respond, but his body language showed that he did not like the way I responded to him. After a few minutes, I saw that he took a knife out of his pocket with a few other tools all joined together by a chain and started to play with them. I knew he was trying to intimidate me.

The bus driver was required to stop at every check point for passengers to be checked by religious guards. The first checking station was at the outskirts of the town. The bus stopped and two guards boarded. One stood at the entrance and the other came to the back of the bus, ordering everyone out. As soon as the boy saw the guards he put his knife back into his pocket.

The passengers were asked to take their belongings with them. We went out and waited in line for the inspection. When my turn arrived a guard led me into a room with a third guard who took my bag from me and went into another room to check its contents. I was questioned by the guard in the room about where I was coming from and why I was turned back. The investigation took longer than usual; I was the last one to get my bag back.

The bus was waiting for me. I rushed into the bus but did not go to my seat. I told the bus driver about the young boy in the bus. I said that if I could not sit in a different place I would get off and wait for another bus. The bus driver gave me one of the front seats. I put my bag in a little space in front of me, between my legs, glad to be away from the boy.

As the driver pulled away from the check point, the boy came forward and asked, "Why did you sit this man beside you? Did he say anything about me?"

The driver said, "Look! This is not an easy driving zone. I have to drive very carefully. One mistake can take the life of all. Why don't you sit in your seat until I pass this area, and then I will answer your question?"

Everybody knew that this area was a dangerous zone. Stopping on this road could result in a robbery. The boy did not go back to his seat. He leaned on the door and glanced at me periodically. The driver also must have been afraid, not wanting to speak to him aggressively. He may have had a gun hidden or friends waiting on the road ahead of the bus.

I relaxed as we approached the next check point, which was a police station. A policeman with a gun in his hand was standing in front of the building. Immediately, I got out of the bus and went to the police, telling him that I was afraid of a possible thief in the bus. "Could you please help me to get another bus going to Tehran?" I asked.

While I was talking to him, the boy got out of the bus, and conveyed through body language that the police should avoid helping me. I pointed out the boy to the policeman, and to my relief, he said, "Stay here beside me. I'll get you on another bus."

The bus driver saw me standing outside and said, "We are going; jump in."

I told him I would take a later bus. The driver knew the boy was a problem but didn't want the police to think he couldn't handle it. So he said, "Don't worry about the boy. He won't hurt you."

"Look!" said the policeman. "We know that you're a good driver. But he is OK. To avoid problems, I'd better send him on another bus."

The bus driver boarded, waiting for the boy to get on. He hesitated but got on, giving me and the policeman fierce looks. Then the bus departed. Within a few minutes, other buses arrived. The policeman knew one of the drivers well and asked him to give me a lift to Tehran. The new driver let me sit beside him saying, "You look very tired. You and your bag are safe here. Nobody can touch you unless he walks over my dead body first. So, have peace of mind and rest as long as you want."

This was a great relief to me. The bus arrived in Tehran the following morning, and I caught another bus to Talesh immediately after that. The following night I arrived home. I called a friend and asked him to come with me to the court, as I was told at the border. I thought if they took me back to prison or wanted something else, my friend would be able to take the message to my family. The following day we went to the court, but the judge did not send me to prison. He asked for bail as a guarantee that I would not leave the city without the permission of the court. Without my asking my friend offered his house as bond, and I was released from the court.

Selling Yogurt

My credibility was waning. I lost my friends and followers. Friendships were not easy to maintain anymore. Fear of the mullahs kept people away from me. Financially, we were in dire straits. I was not allowed to work and for this reason our savings were disappearing fast. Some of our family and friends helped us financially, but this could not continue. If the mullahs knew that they were helping us, it would put them at risk.

Without work, the financial pressure was great, and I had no choice but to take my wife and daughter to our village and live in a little orchard farm with my mother in the house I built for her while I was in government but remained unfinished.

As a city girl, my wife was unable to adapt herself to the hard life in the village and this made our married life calamitous. I desired to end our marriage but this would make the family problems far more complicated. How could I look after our very young daughter without her mother, with poverty, and while uncertain about the future and living day by day?

My 60-year-old mother was poor, managing her life with a milking cow and a small farm. While I was working she did not have financial difficulties. But after I lost everything her life was affected as well. To survive, she sold milk and yogurt, walking 45 minutes from our village to the town to find customers. She became ill and was unable to take her products to the market, so I would do it for her to buy bread for the household. But it was not easy for me to do this because of my fame. I was embarrassed. However, my mother's courage was a good lesson. She did not worry what people thought about her.

Selling milk and yogurt put me at risk politically. I was a famous politician known to thousands of people, who thought I deserved to be one of the leading figures in the country. But now, I was selling yogurt and milk for survival. Many people who saw my mother and I, expressed their unhappiness to us secretly, blaming the mullahs as the cause of our poverty.

The area's authorities interpreted this as a political propaganda against them and told me to stop selling the yogurt. I was an educated man and leader of many people. They didn't want the people to think that the governing mullahs were the cause of my financial hardship.

I was well aware that the mullahs' evil roots were stronger than ever in the country, and I had to avoid any direct opposition with them. When they requested that I stop selling, I told them, "My mother normally sells the yogurt and milk, but at the moment she is sick and I have no choice but to do this for her. I'm just trying to feed my family, not fighting the government. I cannot stop this until my mother is well." I said this and left.

What I was doing was not political propaganda, but the mullahs saw it as a silent war against them. However, they did not take me to prison again; I believe that they were afraid of people and did not want to do so. They also knew that some powerful people were behind my release; who they were, they did not know, but they were aware if they took me to prison they would be face to face with a legal authority more powerful than them. By that time, all my fellow prison inmates and a few other friends had been killed. Local authorities, expecting that I would have been executed by now as well, plotted to kill me secretly and free the community from influence.

Hit by a Truck

One day in 1986, I had sold yogurt, bought bread, and was heading home on foot. The street was lined with small manufacturing businesses. It was the same street where I pleaded the guard several months ago to allow me to see my family for a few minutes while I was being taken to Chalous for my death sentence. Some of my friends and relatives also had businesses there. As I was walking, I realized that a few religious guards were driving back and forth down both sides of the road. They slowed each time they approached me, looking at me strangely. Although I was unnerved, I tried to look unassuming.

As I neared the workshop of a friend, I decided to go in. I told him I thought something may happen to me. He offered to take me home in his car, but I didn't want to cause trouble for him. I was sure that if the guards had an evil plan, they would harm him too.

I left his workshop and continued to walk towards home. A few minutes later, I heard the sound of an accident behind me. I turned around and saw that a guard's SUV was pushing a larger truck onto the sidewalk area so it could hit me. The truck belonged to the city council, and its driver was also a volunteer religious guard. I ran as fast as I could when I saw the truck getting closer to me. In a split second, I decided to throw myself into a deep ditch that ran parallel between the sidewalk and street. However, the truck caught my left foot and twisted me in the air and threw me down into the ditch. Everything went black.

When I opened my eyes, many people gathered around me. My left leg had abrasions, my ankle was dislocated, and my heel was broken. Some people wanted to take me to the hospital, but friends advised against it, afraid that a government agent could kill me by injection and nobody would know it. They took me to my home and brought two traditional doctors to care for me. By the time the doctors arrived, my leg was swollen and black, making the job harder for them and extremely painful for me. As they worked to set the bones, the severe pain caused me to vomit and faint several times.

These doctors did the best they could with their traditional medical care, but for a long time I was unable to stand. It was a year before I was able to walk again. Even then, I limped from the pain.

Blessing in Disguise?

The truck driver who hit me came to my house alone one day. He apologized, saying he was forced to attempt to kill me in partnership with the guard. He was so glad that I did not die. Though the accident disabled me for a year, paradoxically, I gained momentum. The plot of local authorities became clear to everyone, and people realized that it was they who wanted to kill me. This caused me more fame than ever in the eyes of people. The authorities backed off, leaving me alone for a while and, as a result, some fearful friends took a step of courage and rebuilt their relationship with me again.

After I started to walk, a friend offered me a job at his business, but under another name, as it was illegal for me to work. It was a management position, and my salary reflected that. He took such a risk to help me because the local authorities had retreated from their pursuit of me in that time.

This job not only met my family's financial needs, but also enabled me to save money.

Daniel with his family before finding a secure way to leave Iran

165

After several months I bought a tractor and a truck and asked my younger brother to work them, so that I could gain extra income. My brother started to plow lands and carry sand for construction. Our income grew rapidly and I invested in real estate under the name of another friend. Within a year, I became a millionaire, according to the Iranian Riyal. I took my wife and daughter to the city and lived in a rental house. I also started to build a house for my wife in the city. This made my wife happy and eased the tension in our marriage. At this time, she was pregnant with our second child. I also invested in my mother's house and finished it so that my younger brother could live with my mother as an appreciation of his role in making big money through the tractor. My mother did not need to sell milk or yogurt anymore. I made myself busy with investments to make money and also give false confidence to the authorities that I was going to live in Iran and wouldn't want to leave the country.

A Secure Way to Leave

Towards the end of 1987, I started to plan a secure way for me to leave the country. My death sentence was still on me. I believed my friends who released me were delaying the issue of the 'review' of my papers so that I could once again attempt to leave the country. On the other hand, I had become a wealthy man and would have loved to stay alive longer. Life seemed good. My wife and I now had three daughters and I wanted to leave Iran and find a safe place for them to live.

I needed to have my passport back and my name removed from the black list in the ports. I knew that only influential people could accomplish this. At that time, our city was preparing for an election. A few men who gained their legal status from the authorities announced their candidacy for the parliament and began campaigning. It was a good time for me to build a relationship with an influential follower of one of these candidates. This would pave the way for my future needs to be met.

The man I chose acted as a mediator and my passport was released to him from the Revolutionary Court in our city. When I was told that my name would soon be removed from the black list, I rejoiced. Immediately, I took measures to leave the country while the city was busy with the election. I exchanged most of my money for the U.S. dollar.

A friend from another city offered to travel with me to make sure I crossed the border into Turkey. I had $44,000. At that time, passengers had to report foreign currency written in the passport by a bank. I had $22,000 in my passport and the other $22,000 in my friend's passport.

It was the beginning of 1988 when we traveled to the same border from where I was previously sent back. My friend and I were sent to one customs agent, since we were traveling together. He gave his passport first and got the exit stamp. When the agent checked my passport he informed me that I was on the black list and not allowed to leave.

"I was told my name had been removed from the black list," I said.

"I don't know about that. But as long as your name is on the blacklist, you cannot go out."

As he was calling a guard to take care of me, I quickly gave all my money to my friend and said to him, "It seems to me my situation will be harder this time than the previous one. I hope the way they gave the passport to me is not a plot. Otherwise, they can accuse me of a second attempt to escape. Talk to my wife and see if she wants to take the children and leave the country. Also, tell her that she has my consent for anything she wants to do."

The guard took me to the chief guard, who was not as kind as the one I'd met here a couple years before. This man was extremely rude, pointing his pistol to my head and shouting at me. He took my passport, and ordered a guard to bring him the document made under my name when I was returned to my hometown in 1985. Looking at the document, he said, "A second attempt at escape? This is not a lawless country, sir. Who do you think we are? Anti-revolutionaries cannot cross the border. They must be kept inside the country and be persecuted forever for their actions against the Revolution until they understand what justice is."

"I do not want to cross the border illegally," I told him. "I was given my passport back and told that I was free to go out anytime I liked."

"Your name is on the blacklist. You should have checked this first!" he shouted.

"I did, sir. That's why I am here. Could you please do me a favor and call the authorities to confirm this?"

For a few minutes, he said nothing. He called a guard from the next room and asked him to make a phone call and connect the phone to him when someone responded. Then he ordered me to sit on a chair. I was there without any guard beside me. Suddenly, emotions overwhelmed me and tears poured from my eyes. I whispered to myself, "Oh, my painful soul! It seems to me that there is no one to understand you."

The subordinate guard reported to the chief, saying, "I left a message, but no one has called back."

"Wait a bit and try again," he said.

Three times the guard came to the chief guard and reported to him that there had been no response to his calls. At the end, the chief guard went to the guards' room and closed the door. After about five minutes he came to me and said, "We called the Revolutionary Mayor, the Revolutionary Court of your city and the Immigration Office in Tehran, but no one has responded so far. Forgive us for keeping you so long. Please go to customs, get your passport stamped, and enter Turkey. I alerted customs to stamp your passport."

The sudden change in chief's attitude shocked and astonished me. What happened that he became so obliging towards me and allowed me to cross the border with no confirmation from the authorities? Was there a supernatural being around who heard the cry of my heart? Was there a supernatural hand shattering the high wall for me so that I could cross the border? Who knows?

I received my passport and thanked him with bowing down and left. The distance between the chief guard's office and the customs was around hundred yards. I did not have full control over my legs because of fear and shock. I was emotionally gripped in both fear and excitement while I was walking this distance; fear because it was not believable and excitement because if I made it I would be free. It was terrifying for me to turn around and look back and see whether the chief or a guard was watching me. I had learnt in prison when a guard asks you to go, you had to go with all your being focused in going; you never look around. If you do and take notice of the things around you may lose or be shot.

I returned to the same customs agent. He stamped my passport, and I crossed the Iranian border into the Turkish immigration area. My passport was stamped by a Turkish agent too, and I entered Turkey. There I would discover another amazing miracle.

A
NEW
LIFE

10

A New Country

Over the Border

When I stepped into the Turkish immigration office, I remembered that I had given all my money to my friend and had not kept any for myself. But as I left the Immigration Office, I saw my bus and discovered that it had been waiting for me for over two and a half hours. My friend had paid the driver to wait. Some passengers were understandably angry at me for being made to wait so long, but some were happy that I was released and allowed to enter Turkey.

It was night. The driver drove towards Ankara, a twenty-two hour drive. We stopped for breakfast the following morning. My friend and I got out and the first thing I did was to call my wife and let her know that I crossed the border, and I was safe in Turkey. As soon as she heard my voice, she did not allow me to speak. Crying, she told me that the Revolutionary Mayor had called the border and ordered them to return me to our city to face justice. Someone in the Mayor's office called one of my friends, who informed my wife that I was in danger. She wanted to warn me to stay away from the border if I was not already there. She knew that the Revolutionary Mayor was a violent man. He was not a Taleshi, but from Tehran. The mullahs appointed their own leaders in each city. Generally speaking, they do not appoint native men to the important positions, knowing locals favor their own. They appointed merciless people to keep the authoritarian Islamic leadership alive.

"I am in Turkey," I told her. "Do not worry anymore. If they come to ask about me, just say I have told you that I was going somewhere and would come back soon." I did not hear any response. "Hello? Hello?" I thought perhaps my wife had fainted after hearing such unbelievable news. She was OK, only in shock after receiving my news. I was glad to pass the message of my successful escape to her.

Our trip came to an end in Ankara, the capital city of Turkey. My friend and I slept in a hotel that night and the next morning I went to introduce myself at the United Nations' office. They set a date for an interview. If I passed the interview they would send me as a refugee to a western country.

There were many Iranians waiting in front of the United Nations' building. One of them told me that he had secured an apartment with a Taleshi man and there was room for me if I wanted to share the rent with them. I went to his apartment, met the man from my hometown and decided to live with them. They both were members of the *Mujahidin-e Khalgh-e Iran* (MKI). They had finished their interviews with the United Nations and were waiting for the results. The majority of Iranian refugees who had enrolled in the United Nations were the members of MKI.

MKI members in Turkey expected me to join their group and continue fighting against the mullahs of Iran. After Dr Banisadr escaped from Iran, he united with the MKI for a while. Because I was a pro-Dr Banisadr while I was in power in Iran, the MKI members in Turkey expected me to join their party.

I did not wish to get involved in any political activities again, so I refused their request. Unfortunately, this cost me a great deal. They had power in the United Nations in Turkey. Almost all Persian (Farsi) interpreters in the United Nations were members of the MKI, and they had established a strong relationship with some of its interviewers.

On the day of my interview I walked out of the interview room because my interpreter was not honest in the interpretation, twisting my words. The extortion was so obvious that even with knowing a little English I was able to understand it. I informed the interviewer a few times, but he shouted over me and asked me to stop complaining. I eventually said to the interviewer that I had problems with the way I was interviewed, and I was not going to tolerate it. I asked for another interview time with an interpreter who was not a member of MKI. After I said this, I walked out.

I went to the Information Center and reported what had transpired during the interview. He said it was the interviewer's responsibility to arrange another interview. Shortly after the first interview I was granted another with the same interviewer as before, but the interpreter once again turned out to be a member of the MKI.

"Excuse me sir. Don't you remember that I was displeased with the first MKI interpreter and applied for a second interview with a non-MKI member?" I asked.

When the attendant said that he was unable to get a non-MKI interpreter, I told him, "I am sorry that my request was not important to you sir. I will not be able to sit for an interview with an interpreter who is not translating accuratel. This gentleman, along with the previous interpreter, has already threatened my application. So how can you expect me to allow his interpretation?"

I walked out of the United Nations' Office never to return. A week later, I left Ankara and went to Istanbul, where I lived with an Iranian student who was from my city.

After a month, my wife and daughters joined me in Istanbul. Because we had money we did not have financial concerns. We did not know what would happen to us in the future however.

Would we find a country in which to live? Would we stay our entire life in Turkey? If yes, then how?

To get a Turkish visa, you had to have a huge sum of money and start a business. We did not have such money. I decided to learn the language, obtain a student visa, and enter a university. My family would need a dependent visa. If we had these visas we would not need to renew our tourist visa every three months by exiting then re-entering the country across the Turkey and Bulgaria border.

The Turkish language was not so foreign to me. Azeri, the language of my mother and Azerbaijanis, is very close to Turkish and is in the family of Turkic languages. It was the summer of 1988 that I sat for an entry exam for a master's degree in management. I passed the exam, exceeding the standard, and was accepted.

My family applied for a year-long dependent residential visa. However, because we refused to be involved in any bribery and corruption in the application process, our family visa delayed and we received it in the tenth or eleventh month of each year we stayed in Turkey. Since the visas weren't issued to us until October or November of each year, and expired at the end of December, my family did not have visas for the other months of the year. Without a visa, no one was allowed to stay in Turkey for more than 90 days. So every 90 days my wife and children went to the border of Turkey and Bulgaria, entered into Bulgaria five minutes before midnight and returned to Turkey five minutes after midnight, since they could not legally exit and enter Turkey within the same day. It was very hard for a woman with three young children to endure the difficulties of such a journey in the cold, in the middle of the night, and in such an insecure area.

My wife bore this harshness for the entire educational season in 1988-89. The heavy burden of travel and homesickness prompted her to return to Iran with our children in the first half of June 1989. It would be five months before I would see them again.

Betrayed by a Business Partner

I had already built a relationship with an Iranian man who had a small business in Istanbul. At his request, I pooled my money with his and joined him as a business partner. We planned to export Turkish products to Germany. Although I knew nothing about the export business in Turkey, I believed I would learn from him. Our capital totaled US$50,000. While waiting for our import-export license, we decided to get involved with buying and selling anything in the Istanbul market that could provide us with extra money. We got involved in the currency market and continued to make more money.

In July 1989, I informed my partner that I needed time off to prepare for my master's thesis at Istanbul University. He supported my educational pursuit, and because I trusted him, I left my share of capital with him. We spoke a few times during the week, but when I attempted to contact him after receiving my master's degree, he was nowhere to be found. I decided to contact a real estate friend of his I had met previously.

When I told him what had happened, his words shocked me. "He may have taken the money and left. Honestly, I do not know where he is." At his suggestion, I checked with my partner's travel agent, who informed me that my partner had gone to Germany. The news was overwhelming as I contemplated bankruptcy and a bleak future for my family.

I didn't know what to do. From the real estate agent I received the phone number of my partner's wife, who was in Germany visiting relatives at the time. When I reached her she told me that her husband had been caught with drugs and was in prison. She apologized and said she would try to inform the police and perhaps get some of my money returned. In my heart, I did not trust her words.

I went to the German Consulate in Istanbul and to the International Police Bureau for help, but with no documentation of our partnership or my share of the money, there was nothing they could do. The company was registered in my partner's name initially and I was not able to prove that I was his legal business partner. Also, I could not get a visa nor did I have money to travel to Germany.

What little money I had would be gone soon. I needed to work but had enrolled at the university to earn a PhD. Part-time work would not be enough to support my family. The situation was extremely distressing.

I recalled that there was an Iranian Christian group who came to my business partner and he also attended their church in Istanbul sometimes. I decided to go there to see if anyone had any knowledge of his whereabouts. The church had an outreach to Iranian refugees, and my partner had received help there. I had learned about this when I visited his home and saw a Bible in the Persian language sitting on his coffee table. Startled that I had seen it, my partner said that, although he thought it was a good book, he didn't believe in it. He was a Muslim and would stay a Muslim.

To have this book in his possession was illegal in Islam. That's why he showed nervous when I saw the book.

He told me that the church consisted of Christians who were afraid to live in Iran after the Revolution. Many had been Muslims but now were followers of Jesus.

I was shocked. "Muslims became Christians? How can this be?" I asked him.

"Whether you believe it or not, they say that they have left Islam behind, and they are Christians now. Not only that but they are brave, too, since the penalty for apostasy in Islam is death," he said.

"How can Muslims leave a perfect and civilized religion and go back to an uncivilized one? Christianity is 600 years older than

Islam, and Islam came to perfect the defects of Christianity," I said. Even though I had lost my zeal for Islam, this was what I was supposed to say as a Muslim after learning that he had been in their church.

He offered to take me to talk to someone at the church but I refused. "I have escaped from one death sentence. I do not want another one," I said, "Please leave me out of this. How did you come to know these people?"

"They have helped a lot of Iranian refugees here in Turkey" he replied. "They don't hesitate to help anyone. Last Christmas, they invited many Iranians to their Christmas party, and I was one of them. At the end of the party, they gave the Bible to me as a gift."

"Wow!" I said. "They are brave."

Secretly, I wanted to go and learn why these people left Islam and joined Christianity, but I was afraid to express myself to him. I was schooled in Islam and was familiar with its intolerance towards other religions. I knew that any soft approach toward Christianity could expose me to the danger of Islamic punishment. Though I was backslidden from the practices of Islam and was living as a nominal Muslim, I kept my thoughts to myself in order to protect myself from possible danger as much as I could.

One day, while we were going to the Bazaar in Istanbul, my business partner showed me the church. It was an old, beautiful building on a hilly area. I saw some graffiti on the wall of the church, left by radical Muslims who wanted it closed.

However, after my business partner had taken my money and escaped, I decided to go to that church to inquire about him. For the first time in my life I was going to a Christian church. I felt very uncomfortable; this was a zone prohibited by Islam. At any time, radical Muslims could enter the church and shoot everybody, including me. Besides, I wanted to keep a low profile because of my heavy involvement with the

Iranian Revolution and my escape. I did not want the church members to know that I was a radical Muslim and a fugitive. Most Iranians in Turkey kept their lives secret. Turkey was not a safe place for Iranians who were ex-politicians or fugitives. The terrorists of the Islamic Republic of Iran were spread everywhere in Turkey and they killed many fugitive politicians in Turkey.

My business partner had told me that some Iranians had lied to these Christians, receiving financial aid from them when they did not need it. I was concerned they may not believe I had lost my money. So, as I stood in front of the church, I changed my mind and did not go inside. As I left, I realized I had to do something to bring back the money I had lost. I decided to enter the church. Despite my reservations I entered the church yard and knocked on the door. An elderly lady answered and asked, "Who are you looking for?"

When I told her I was there to visit someone from the Iranian Church, she said that they would be there Sunday afternoon. So I returned on Sunday. As I was entering the church, I saw people playing musical instruments in front of a crowd. People were standing, singing and lifting their hands. This was a shocking sight to me. Music is evil in Islam, especially in a place of worship.[1] Committed Muslims never listen to any music. I was shocked even more when I saw ladies were also singing and raising their voices among men and in a worship place. Immediately I thought, Wow! This is one reason that Islam is called superior to Christianity.

---

1   Muhammad said: Allah commanded him to destroy all the musical instruments, idols, crosses and all the trappings of ignorance (*Hadith Qudsi* 19:5). Allah Mighty and Majestic sent me as a guidance and mercy to believers and commanded me to do away with musical instruments, flutes, strings, crucifixes, and the affair of the pre-Islamic period of ignorance. On the Day of Resurrection, Allah will pour molten lead into the ears of whoever sits listening to a songstress (*Umdat al-Salik* r40.0).

I had grown up with music my entire life. My father, a nominal Muslim, listened to music on his radio. He himself had a beautiful voice, singing from time to time in gatherings with his friends or on the farm. My mother's brother was an Azeri musician and made his income playing at weddings and other celebrations. My mother is an Azeri. Music is interwoven into Azeri's culture and life style.

Music has accompanied the meaningful messages (poems) of Persians and Azeri's forefathers for generations. I loved music, but had put it away because the Islamic Republic of Iran prohibited it. Despite my early connection to music, I had never seen or heard of it in a worship context. When I saw the congregation participating in music, my immediate thought was 'sin'.

I stayed aloof, sitting in the back of the church. I was afraid that if a Muslim came in and saw me standing, he would accuse me of participating in this evil practice with Christians. I had enough problems and did not want to provide grounds for further accusation by the Iranian authorities or other Muslims. I sat behind the people closest to the main door, thinking if something strange happened I could easily run away.

When the singing stopped, a Turkish Christian was introduced to the crowd and asked to preach. He spoke in Turkish and someone interpreted it into Persian for those Iranians who did not know Turkish. Since I understood both languages, I heard the message twice. But I wasn't paying attention. All I could think of was my business partner and how I wanted to kill him.

When the service was over, a few people welcomed me warmly. I told them the story of my loss and they offered to help, saying they would do their best to find my partner in Germany and try to get back my money or at least some of it. They said that they had many Christian friends in Germany, and through them, they would be able to find and contact him. They asked me to keep in touch with them so that I could be informed of any news from Germany. I asked them how I could keep in touch. They said, "Keep coming to the church, the best place to see each other frequently." This was not good news since I was afraid to go to church. I was expecting them to see me somewhere else and inform me of the news. However, reluctantly I responded that it will be OK, but in my heart the response was 'no'.

Going to Church

Because of my fear, I decided not to go to the church anymore. Then I thought that if I did not go they would think that I had given up, and they would not ask their friends in Germany to search for my business partner. So I began attending the church every Sunday with fear. In the first couple of weeks I decided not to pay attention to what they were preaching. I thought that their words might influence me and cause problems for me with Islam. But they were such nice, kind people. Because of their loving attitude, I was not able to cover my ears any longer. As soon as I started to listen to their messages my assumption about Christians and their teaching began to change. I heard amazing philosophical, doctrinal and moral things which I had never heard before.

I thought I was going to the church for my money, but God sent me there for a different reason. The world of Islam had framed me into a world of misinformation, selfishness, religious nationalism, discrimination, and racism. I was amazed how these Christians' teachings were so different to what we were taught of Christians. They were all talking about God and showed a great reverence to God. They read the Bible, prayed, and sang to God all in their own mother tongues. In Islam you have to pray to Allah in Arabic, a language that you do not know, but have just memorized some words in order to repeat them daily. It occurred to me if God is the Creator of all nations, and is mighty and all-knowing, He would know their languages and speak to them through their languages.

Why would He give them a hard time and push them to communicate with Him via a strange language?

I was also amazed by their modesty. Muslims are taught that Christians are the most immoral and ungodly people in the world and their women are whores because they do not cover themselves in an Islamic way.[2] I was shocked to see how lovely, godly and modest these people were. I thought, Why do we call this respectful life 'ungodliness' and 'immoral'? I saw such a contrast between the behavior of Christian men toward their wives and the treatment of women in Islam. We humiliated our wives and beat them, according to the instruction of the Quran and Islam,[3] and called it moral and godly, but in contrast we called the sincere love and friendliness of these Christians to their spouses immoral.

Is it moral if we, as the Quran instructs, lock our wives in a room or force them to be indistinguishable, covering their faces anytime they go outside? [4] Is it moral to call our wives lesser[5] than us, that they are our properties[6] and only men are able to fulfill God's requirements?[7]

I continued to search for the responses to these questions as I compared myself and my beliefs with these Christians. I was shocked by the answers I found. The followers of Christ had no right to do such things to their wives.

I never heard a curse word from them. They said lying is lying no matter who the opposite party might be. We learned from the Quran and Islam that lying for the sake of Allah was

---

2   In his comments on Q33:59, Ibn Khathir, the renowned Islamic scholar, says in his commentary that uncovered women are servants or whores.

3   Q4:34; 38:44.

4   Q4:15; 33:33, 59.

5   Q2:228, 282; 4:11, 176.

6   Q53:2.

7   Q33.

legitimate and moral.[8]How could we Muslims call Christians immoral for avoiding any kind of lie, no matter to friend or foe, and believing that God rejects all kinds of lies?

Another thing that amazed me was the belief in unconditional love or loving and respecting people unconditionally. It is the unconditional love that removes the barrier among people, they taught. This was so different to the teachings of Allah, who cannot tolerate unconditional love. Not only did he not love humanity but also designed and created calamity and pain for them[9] and created them sinners[10]. What kind of love can it be if someone gives you pain, corrupts you and rids you of choice?

We were taught to disrespect Christians and destroy their interests as much as we could, yet these Christians were taught to love us. My mind was reeling. "Am I dreaming?" I said to myself. We followed the Quran and called Christians the worst of beasts, unclean, ungodly, infidels and unloving but they were teaching and practicing unconditional love. They were not just lovely in words, but also in deeds. They had every right to reject me because of my background, but they didn't. I found the difference between the teaching of Islamists and these Christians was the difference between darkness and light. I remembered the poems of one of our renowned thirteenth century poets, Mowlana Rumi who said:

> *The love of the infidels drew my attention,*
> *and because of that I am now smooth (loving), gentle and*
> *simple.*

He is criticizing Muslim nations for calling infidels unlovely, whereas their love changed him totally. Now, I was able to understand the meaning of his call that Muslims need to learn valuable things from the so-called infidel Christians.

---

8   Q2:225; 3:28; 16:106 & *Reliance of the Traveller*, P.745.

9   Q57:22.

10 Q91:7-8.

Not only were these Christians' relational values amazing, their doctrine and philosophy of God were also amazing. They were teaching that God was personal; He could reveal Himself to people to establish a personal relationship with them and save them from the bondage of Satan. They were claiming that they were saved, united with God and His ambassadors on earth in order to reveal God's plan to people and lead them to His light.

Their messages were challenging, and I found truth in their description of God as the personal God and Savior. In the midst of meditation on their words, I said to myself, "Of course, if God is absolutely just, holy, loving, and living, He must present Himself as the ultimate authority in all these good things and equip us so that we are enabled to live them and use them in our relationship with others. If God is called the role model, He must be a personal and revealing God in order to become the role model for personal humanity." This was a new and powerful philosophical discovery for me that God is personal, everywhere and able to have personal relationship with everybody. He is a living God for living people and for an actual relationship.

My heart desired to be rid of spiritual slavery since God was around. "If lawlessness is a reality, if Satan exists," I said to myself, "then I absolutely desire to be released from his bondage and influence." But how? Without verbalizing my question, I received the answer through the teaching of the Christians:

There are two spiritual kingdoms in the world: The Kingdom of God and the kingdom of Satan. You cannot be dependent on both at the same time; your dependency on one means that you are separated from the other. Satan and God have opposite qualities and cannot live with each other. God is light and holy, Satan is dark and unholy. If you belong to the darkness, you cannot be in the light. In the same way, if you have the citizenship of light, you do not belong to the darkness. Darkness and light cannot co-exist.

If you belong to Satan's kingdom, you cannot save yourself. Satan is your king, has power over you, and does not believe in freedom. If you do not call on God, who is mightier than Satan, you will not be able to release yourself. God has given you freedom of choice to decide to live with Satan or call on Him to release you from Satan.

This time, I remembered another of Mowlana's poems:

> *For sure, all are captive to death,*
> *a captive is not able to release you from prison.*

I was so amazed on how God had left this great witness in my culture among Iranians. Mowlana must have read the Gospel of Christ in order to be able to come up with such a Christian philosophy, instead of the expected Islamic philosophy.

The philosophy and logic of the Christians was very influential to me. What is happening here? What am I hearing here? I loved what they were teaching, but I did not express it to anyone. I was afraid that if I verbalized my agreement, they could take it as confirmation that I believed all of what they were teaching, which I didn't. They called Jesus God and the Son of God. And they spoke much about Jews. Allah and Muhammad and Islamic scholars dislike and curse Christians for this. They believe that Christians have made a man (Jesus) as God for themselves and made Jesus equal to God.

The truth was that Muhammad and his followers were unable or unwilling to understand the Christian belief that man was unable to elevate himself or someone else to the position of God, but that God was able to reveal Himself in any form, just as He did in manifesting Himself in Jesus.

I was still unable to understand why Jesus was the only way to heaven. If Muhammad was to come after Him, then Jesus could not be the only way. Even though Muhammad was unsure of his own spiritual destination after death and unable to proclaim himself as the way, he still maintained that he was the only one to lead others to perfection. For this reason, his successors and followers felt obligated to gather the entire world under the umbrella of Islam despite the cost.

Since the cultural atmosphere among Islamic communities is always hostile towards Christians' beliefs, I was afraid of my relationship with Christians who called Jesus the God and the Son of God. The Quran not only rejects the deity of Christ and curses Christians for such a belief; it also forbids Muslims to listen to their teachings or become their friends[11].

Every time these Christians opened the Bible, I heard about Jews. I was brought up in a way to hate Jews. As a Muslim, it was so dangerous for you to keep quiet if you hear anything nice about Jews. Since childhood, I had learned that Jews were the worst among all non-Muslims. The only solution for them was death. Muslims were obligated to clean the world of Jews; the last day would not approach until all Jews were killed according to the instruction of Muhammad[12]. At the university in Iran I became a real hater of Jews because of the instructions of the Quran and Islam. Iranians call themselves Aryan proudly. Hitler's philosophy of hatred and anti-Semitism had a major influence on some radical Iranian Muslims, including myself, who believed that Allah had ordained Iranian Aryans, in a similar way he did with Hitler, to hate and kill Jews and erase them from the surface of the earth.

My mind and heart were corrupted with this hatred and the fear behind it, and it was not easy to see myself among a group of Christians who loved Jews like any other people. I was struggling in my inner being. Although I was moved by some messages, there was still a fear of getting involved with Christians. "Is this going to establish another death sentence for me?" I thought to myself. However, the belief of this Christian group was always challenging me:

---

11 Q3:118

12 *Muslim*:: Book 41:: Hadith 6985 & *Bukhari*:: Volume 4:: Book 52: Hadith 177.

> *Do not be afraid of those who kill the body but cannot kill the soul. Rather, be afraid of the one who can destroy both soul and body in hell.* (Matthew 10:28)

In other words, stand for the truth even if it costs you your life. The truth rules only with the sacrifices of truth-loving people.

Would I Dare to Stand for the Truth?

One day when alone in my rented flat in Istanbul, I saw myself as a man who had faced only difficulties. Sadness overcame me like a heavy weight as I recounted all the bad events which had occurred throughout my life. The world and everything in it, including myself, seemed unjust. I turned my face up to heaven and cried out to God? "Why don't you help me? I know that you are mighty and can help me."

I was so angry at God. I wanted Him to appear to me so that I could hit Him, believing He was the reason for my pain. Why should I carry such burdens when there was a mighty Creator who was able to save and comfort me? From the depth of my heart, I believed that there was a God and that He could help me, but I thought that He was ignoring me. In the midst of these emotional moments, my conscience started to raise its critical view; which God are crying to, to Allah or the God of the Bible; to an impersonal God or the personal God; to a god who does not have an ear to hear or to the one who has an ear?

It was amazing that my conscience was counseling me to cry to a God who is personal, has ears and listens. It was telling me that Islam was a barrier between me and my Creator and Savior since it does not believe in any personal relationship between God and humanity. I didn't know that my cries in Islam were futile, since I was not crying to the true God. How could I cry and express my personal agony and anger to an impersonal God? An impersonal god would not be able to understand my personal needs and relate to me personally. So, the pain in my heart and the tears of my eyes taught me meaningful lessons and directed me to the true and living

God. The moment was very logical and also ripe for lifting my eyes to heaven sincerely and meaningfully. It was the first time in my life that I was seeing the necessity of an immediate touch and healing from God, believing He could reveal Himself to me personally and help me.

The following night I had a dream. There were earthquakes and violent winds. People were running and crying. Houses were demolished and many people were killed. I was in my father's house, alone. It was the same house in which I grew up. In my dream, I stayed in the open room at the front of the old house and cried out to God, "Why don't you help me? I am alone here."

Immediately after my cry, a light appeared in the sky and said, "I am Jesus. Come out of your father's old house. Be not afraid, I will help you." So I rushed out of my father's house and ran toward an apple tree in the front yard which the light showed me. I fell to the ground and turned as the old house fell down. When I awoke, the startling dream kept me from falling back to sleep.

The events in the dream began to occupy my mind. I wondered if something was going to happen to me. I was rescued, but my father's house was destroyed. Did the dream mean that I was safe outside my country, but my other family members, including my wife and children, were going to die?

I also started to question God's response to my cry. I thought that I had asked for help but he destroyed my old house. In the Middle East, the expression of the deepest pain of your life is verbalized by the saying, "my house was ruined". Was I going to face more difficulties and experience more pain in the future? In the following days I was filled with anxiety, I prepared myself for bad news.

The next Sunday I went to the church, still hoping for news of my money. What I heard shocked and amazed me. The title of the sermon was *The House on the Rock of Jesus* (Luke 6:48f).

The preacher spoke of the things that I had seen and heard in my dream. He was calling the congregation to newness of life:

Leave your old house; leave your father's house. Your old house is the house of sin, the house of your selfish desire and the house of your old nature that you have inherited from Adam. It is a house built on sand, which is easily destroyed. Come out, leave it otherwise it will collapse on you. Come and live in the house that Christ has built for you on the Rock. Nothing can destroy this house, because it is the house of absolute freedom, joy and peace. Christ is the Prince of glory, peace and love. His unconditional love has lifted Him up, soaring on high like an eagle. He wants to establish you on this higher ground. This is the ground where Satan cannot reach. It is the ground of God, the ground of salvation and victory over all inhuman and ungodly attitudes and values. Come to Him; do not ignore His call.

What is happening here? I thought. I wasn't sure if it was real or if I was having another dream. The words of the sermon completely captivated me. But I said nothing. I still had reservations about being seen with Christians. And I still wanted my money. But inside, I felt different. I decided to read the Bible to see if anything in it related to my dream or to the words of the preacher.

On the way home, the message "Come out from your old house and live in the house of Jesus" replayed in my mind over and over. I understood that it referred to spiritual newness. This idea of newness was not strange to me, as I had delved into mystic and poetic philosophy. They spoke of newness and unity with God, each without their own type of doctrine and theory. As I repeated the call of the preacher in my mind, I was becoming more interested in reading the Gospel to see if it supported a different kind of unity. If yes, I thought, then this has to be a new philosophy that I am not aware of.

From reading the first pages of the Gospel, I was amazed. I discovered that, unlike all other religions, the salvation of humanity and the establishment of God's Kingdom in their hearts is a present reality, not left for the life after. The Gospel proclaims the personal presence of God among people. Those who recognize the presence of God and open themselves to Him receive the Kingdom of God in their hearts.

The kingdom of heaven is near. (Matthew 3:2; 4:17)

The kingdom of God is within you. (Luke 17:21)

Unlike the God of the Bible, Allah in Islam is not a personal God able to have a personal relationship with his people or establish his kingdom in their hearts. He did not reveal himself even to his own apostle and messenger, Muhammad. If he did not reveal himself to Muhammad and did not talk to him personally, how then could Muhammad talk about him without knowing him personally? You need to know someone in order to be able to talk about him. So the Gospel was opening my mind to understand that Allah could not be relevant to life if he was impersonal, unable to talk personally and relate himself to humanity.

As I was meditating on this issue, I gradually started to doubt Allah's existence. Muslims say that Allah asked the angel Gabriel to convey his message (the Quran) to Muhammad rather talking to him personally. This also appeared to me a wrong philosophy. If Gabriel was able to reveal himself to Muhammad, he would be a personal (revealing) being. How then could impersonal (non-revealing) Allah reveal himself to the personal Gabriel and send him as his personal ambassador to Muhammad? It is impossible for an impersonal being to have a personal relationship with a personal being. Also, the impersonal god cannot talk, because he does not have a mouth. We cannot attribute any head, mouth, ear, eye, hand or leg to an impersonal god since he is non-revealing, unknowable and indescribable by human vocabulary. Also, no one can see an impersonal god or hear from him, so how could Gabriel describe him?

The whole authority of the Quran concerning the existence of Allah came under question in my mind. Also, since Allah did not reveal himself to Muhammad and did not talk to him personally, where then could the Quran come from? How could it be the instructions of the personal God for the personal needs of humankind? It cannot be anything but Muhammad's own personal words.

My mind was trying to bring everything of Islam to the surface and evaluate it under the light of Gospel's philosophy of God, even though I had not given my heart to it yet. I said to myself, "what about if a Muslim believes that Allah is personal, but he decided not to reveal himself", as I heard this from some back in Iran. To this, my response was clear: "A just God does not hide Himself against the injustice of Satan if He is the ultimate authority in justice." A personal God reveals Himself in order to save and protect people from Satan. If Islam does not believe that salvation must take place in life on earth then it is not a true religion. For Christ, a just, holy and loving God must not ignore people's cry for salvation. Such indifference means co-operation with Satan. God must stand for justice.

I tell you, this was a good tasting revelation. The words of the Gospel began to seem so real, true, delicious and attractive to me. One by one, the beliefs to which I had been in bondage began to dissipate. I realized that an impersonal god does not exist; therefore the act of creation cannot be attributed to him. He is a man-made god. The God of the universe must be personal and in touch with His creatures.

I paused repeatedly as I pondered the wonder of such amazing revelations. Alone in my rented apartment, I was free to revel in my amazement but still hesitant to share my convictions with anyone. The Scriptures were powerfully eye opening and functioned like a living teacher as I read. The first chapter of the Gospel of John was one of them:

In the beginning was the Word, and the Word was with God, and the Word was God. He was in the beginning with God. All things were made through Him; and without him nothing was made that was made. In Him was life, and the life was the light of men. … And the Word became flesh and dwelt among us. We beheld His glory, the glory as of the only begotten of the Father, full of grace and truth. (John 1:1-4, 14)

I already knew that God (or the Ultimate Reality) in each religion was called "the Word," but I did not know that the Word could reveal Himself in human flesh to demonstrate His heavenly glory and truth personally, setting a standard among humanity. I did not know that no human authority could establish the truth of God on earth better than God Himself if they were not the supreme authority of the truth? Therefore, until "the Word" manifests and makes Himself conceivable no one will be able to reach freedom. He revealed Himself in the flesh in order to prepare the way for the freedom of soul-bearers.

The revelation of God amazed me more than before as I read the following passages in the Gospel after understanding John chapter one:

This is my servant whom I have chosen, the one I love in whom I delight; I will put my Spirit on him, and he will proclaim justice to the nations. He will not quarrel or cry out; no one will hear his voice in the streets. A bruised reed he will not break, and a smoldering wick he will not snuff out, till he leads justice to victory. In his name the nations will put their hope. (Matthew 12:18-21)

The reason the Son of God appeared was to destroy the devil's work (1 John 3:8b), and create peace among nations and between nations and God (Colossians 1:20)

My aversion to the Christians' proclamation of Jesus as God was solved. I realized He was not a man-made god. Jesus was God, the Word, and the Spirit who revealed Himself in the flesh in order to be accessible, known and loved. God came to mankind in Jesus in order to redeem, sustain and guide them till the end. In contrast, gods in other religions expect mankind to seek them. Neither a personal man is able to go to an impersonal god nor is an impersonal god able to receive a personal man. In addition, man cannot unchain himself from the prison of Satan, and go to God, since Satan is mightier than man, and does not believe in his freedom. Everything was telling me that the true God is the God who comes and frees people from Satan.

My misunderstanding about Jesus being the Son of God was fully removed as I read the Gospels. The accusation of the Quran is fully irrelevant. The Gospel never says that Jesus is the Son as a result of a sexual relationship between God and Mary. The Sonship of Jesus is fully spiritual and describes His heavenly identity and citizenship. In the same way, the followers of Jesus are called the children of God:

> *You are no longer foreigners and aliens, but fellow citizens with God's people and members of God's household...in which God lives by his Spirit.* (Ephesians 2:19,22)

> *For you did not receive a spirit that makes you a slave again to fear, but you received the Spirit of sonship. And by him we cry," Abba, father." The Spirit himself testifies with our spirit that we are God's children. Now if we are children, then we are heirs—heirs of God and co-heirs with Christ, if indeed we share in his sufferings in order that we may also share in his glory.* (Romans 8:15-17)

The identity of the followers of the heavenly Jesus is heavenly too. For this spiritual citizenship, they are called the children of God.

While reading Apostle Paul's letters, Allah disappeared completely from my heart and was replaced by the holy God through Paul's amazing knowledge of God:

> *Sin entered the world through one man* (Romans 5:12), *through the disobedience of the one man the many were made sinners ...* (v.19)

For since death is through man, the resurrection of the dead also is through a Man. For as in Adam all die, even so in Christ all will be made alive. (1 Corinthian 15:21-22)

Man, not God, is the creator of sin and the cause of humanity's downfall in the Bible. In Islam, Allah is the creator of sin and lawlessness. The Qur'an says that every misfortune and disaster on earth and in the human soul is ordained by Allah[13]; Satan was corrupted by Allah[14]; sin was inspired by Allah in humankind[15]; Allah created man in toil and trouble[16]; Allah leads astray[17].

I had never read and never wanted to read the Qur'an in Persian, because it was taught that no one could understand the words of Allah and therefore it would be better off to recite it in Arabic. Also Allah's preferred language was Arabic and he only accepted the daily Islamic prayers in Arabic. We wanted to align ourselves with Allah's will and read the Qur'an in Arabic if we wished to receive his blessings. This caused us to miss many contradictions in the Qur'an or we would sometimes ask ourselves why would a holy God create sin and corrupt people?

Without knowing Allah, we called him just and holy. Can a just and holy God create sin? No. Isn't creating sin, sin itself? Yes. If Allah is the cause of every misfortune, disaster and unrighteous act, what would you expect his followers to do? It is natural that they will follow the example of Allah. Doesn't the sin inspired by Allah affect Muslims' spiritual, social, moral, political and economic life? It does. If Allah has inspired sin, then can the call of Allah upon his followers be practical and lead them to righteousness and peace with others? Not at all.

---

13 Q57:22.
14 Q7:16.
15 Q91:7-8.
16 Q90:4.
17 Q4:88; 14:4.

I never knew that the God of the Bible was different to Allah. But now, after going to the church, I started to learn the difference that Satan was the creator of sin, not God.[18] Adam and Eve followed Satan and brought sin into the life of humanity, not God. In the Bible, angels and mankind are created with free will. Satan, Adam, and Eve chose to abuse their free will and disobey God.[19] Their rebelliousness is called sin. The God of the Bible is holy and just. Holiness cannot create sin; a just God cannot bear or tolerate sin or have fellowship with sin.

I learnt that a holy God inspires holiness in the heart of humans to have peace with Him and one another[20]. God used Paul, a former radical Jew who condemned and persecuted Christians, in the life of a Muslim, me, who was once radical and hated Christians and Jews. Paul's words made it clear to me that hatred between Muslims and Jews did not come from the holy God, rather from humanity. Unless we are saved and established in the purity of God, we will not be able to reconcile to one another:

> *Hate what is evil; cling to what is good.* (Romans 12:9)
> *Bless those who persecute you, bless do not curse.* (v.14)

Or James says in his letter:

> *The wisdom that comes from heaven is first of all pure; then peace-loving, considerate, submissive, full of mercy and good fruit, impartial and sincere.* (James 1:17)

This was the lesson I learnt in order to unclothe myself from the hatred of Islam and approach Jews with peace. I realized that the root of my hatred for Jews was because I was not united with the pure God and, therefore, was unable even to imagine having peace with Jews. It was here that my heart sensed Jesus as the bearer of God's full glory and set a standard of love and

---

18 Genesis 3
19 Genesis 3; Isaiah 14:12-15; Ezekiel 28:12-19; Jude 6; Revelation 14:6
20 Colossians 1:20.

care for people. Allah is not able to reconcile Muslims and Jews, but Christ can. If Allah is not able to then so are his followers. For decades, the world's superpowers tried to solve the conflict between Palestinians and Jews, but not only were they unable to reconcile the two sides they fueled the hostility between them more and more. Why? First, the values of Christ have been missing there and second, Islam was never understood clearly. The problem of the Middle-East is at the root of Islam that has sanctioned hatred for Jews.

I learnt from the Gospel that   if the root is holy, so are the branches (Romans 11:16). If God is holy, a peacemaker, righteous, loving, and joyful, so are His followers. The root of a belief lies in its God and central philosophies. We embody the characteristics of our root. The root supplies nutrition for the branches and the branches are dependent on the root. The root of Islam is Allah. If Allah has inspired sin, which is stealing, lying, adultery, hatred, killing and debauchery in his followers then his call upon his followers cannot lead to peace and truth. Peace and truth cannot be from the creator of sin. For this reason, unless Muslims turns away from Allah, they will not be able to have a just and peaceful relationship with others.

As a Muslim, I did not have the opportunity to investigate whether my root (Allah) was pure and true. Islam did not allow me to compare it with other religions. I, therefore, was ignorant and did not know whether my religion was logical or achievable. God brought me out from Iran so that I could discover Islam's impracticality and replace it with the truth.

When I finished the New Testament, I read it again. I then read the Old Testament and other Christian books that were available. Reading Exodus 12:22[21] in the Old Testament, I was amazed, heartbroken and then humbled as I remembered

---

21 *And you shall take a bunch of hyssop, dip it in the blood that is in the basin, and strike the lintel and the two door posts with the blood that is in the basin.*

this exact religious practice in my hometown, Talesh. Some Muslim Taleshis, including my family, marked a cross on the top and both sides of the door frame with the blood of sacrificed animals or birds. Were these people Jews in the past, but kept it secret because of their fear of Muslims and then gradually lost their beliefs? This is possible because Jews lived in Iran since the time of Cyrus and Darius the great. Islam asks Jews and Christians, who live among Muslim communities, not to manifest their religion publicly. It asks the males to clip the front of their heads as a shameful sign for being Jew or Christian.[22] Some Taleshi Muslims practiced clipping the front of their heads. Interestingly, some of them also had Jewish names that are not popular among Muslims.

By this time my belief in Islam was destroyed. I had valid reasons why God had to reveal Himself through Christ and why revelation makes the God of the Bible superior to gods in other religions, including Allah. Now I needed to gain a complete understanding for the superiority of Christ's social, political and moral values. So I read the Gospels again, drawn to the root of Islam and Christianity.

While I was amazed by the author of Christian faith, I similarly was also amazed by His relational values for all foes and friends. Jesus says:

Love your enemies and pray for those who persecute you. (Matthew 5:44)

When I heard this for the first time in the church, I was not able to digest it. Islam had taught me that the enemy could not be loved. Islamic culture was alive in me, functioning in me as the root of disbelief. But now, I had to discover them one by one, get rid of them and get myself established in the unconditional love of Christ. Nothing was more influential than His unconditional love to me; while I was His enemy, aiming to destroy His churches and replace them with mosques, He still loved me and gave His life for me. This was

---

22 Al-Turtushi, *Siraj al-Muluk*, pp. 229-230.

His approach to an enemy like me. His unconditional love was not a theory for me anymore; it worked on me so that I could approach my enemies with His logic, reason, love and respect, and encourage them to share these beauties with me.

It was so humbling to me that God of the Bible did not rush into judgment, to deal with me according to my hostile background. He rather invited me to reason with Him, so I could discover the root of the problems in my life. In other words, His love and grace directed His justice to reveal Satan, the root problem, in me and with my consent destroy him, rather than destroying myself. He had created me for Himself and I was so precious to Him. From the depth of my heart, I sensed His true compassion and realized how He was different to Allah. It was here that I was convicted and decided to put the hatred of Islam behind me, and throw myself into the ocean of Christ's love and to pray for my enemies. The words of the Gospel opened my eyes to understand that in God's eyes there are no differences between me and my enemies. Both of us have broken the heart of God and are in need of his grace and love and forgiveness.

In a similar way, I realized that men and women are the same in the eyes of God. They are created by the same God and have the capacity to search, understand, compare and choose. Simply physical appearance cannot make one lesser or greater than the other. Man is not given more than woman or woman than man, especially when it comes to spirituality. God is Spirit and relates Himself to humanity via their spiritual channel, heart. In the spiritual arena, the heart is not defined by gender. Therefore it is wrong, dehumanizing and ungodly when Islam calls females deficient in their identity, understanding or deeds. God created man and woman in order to describe unity and love strongly and supernaturally, not because one is better or has more than the other.

The definition of relationship between a husband and wife in the Gospel was amazing to me. The Gospel says that the unity and love between husband and wife have to be similar to what it is among the members of one body (or flesh)[23]; they have to act sacrificial towards each other as Christ did to His church.[24]

To me, this was the most beautiful way of defining unity. It seemed very true to me. I was thirty-three years old when I read these passages in the Gospel. I confirmed the truthfulness of this logic by using my own body as an example. In the entire thirty three years of my life I never realized for a single moment that my hands reject my feet or my eyes reject my ears. They loved each other and worked with each other harmoniously. In a body, if a member rejects the other, it means that this member is paralyzed and can no longer function in harmony with the others. The body with a paralyzed member is sick. With a similar logic, a family will not be healthy if the husband or wife does not have a unifying and loving faith. If the values of a society are not able to unite people together, that society cannot function as a cohesive and healthy society.

More reading and meditation on the words of the Bible revealed to me the superiority of faith in Christ to all other beliefs and philosophies. I decided to put His life giving words into practice and get myself released from any kind of self-centeredness or hostility:

1. *Love the Lord your God with all your heart and with all your soul and with all your mind.* (Matthew 22:37)

2. *Love your neighbor as yourself.* (Matthew 22:39)

3. *Love your enemies and pray for those who persecute you.* (Matthew 5:44)

4. *Love your wife, just as Christ loved the church and gave himself up for her.* (Ephesians 5:25)

5. *There is neither Jew nor Greek, slave nor free, male nor female, for you are all one in Christ Jesus.* (Galatians 3:28)

---

23 Ephesians 4:16; 5:3.
24 Ephesians 5:24-25;1 Corinthians 12:12.

Who has carried such qualities for life throughout history as Jesus has? Which religion or belief teaches such an unconditional love and includes all in its love no matter of their gender, race or ethnicity? The response was clear to me; Christ was the only One who brought down the walls of separation and united people with each other. He is truly the Lord of lords and the King of kings.[25] The lords and kings of the world were not able to create such a peace among people, but Christ is able to bring people from all nations and races in order to make them the loving members of one body. He brought me out of darkness and hatred, and established me in His peace. The only being hated in the kingdom of Christ is Satan[26], who separates people from one another. You cannot hate Satan unless you love God and humanity and desire to unite with them.

There were times that I asked myself, "Why would a person like Jesus with all these good qualities be hated and crucified?" The response that I found to this question in the Bible broke my heart and brought tears into my eyes:

> He was despised and rejected by men, a man of sorrows, and familiar with suffering. Like one from whom men hide their faces he was despised, and we esteemed him not...He was assigned a grave with the wicked, and with the rich in his death though he had done no violence, nor was any deceit in his mouth. (Isaiah 53:3, 9)

Why would men hide their faces from Jesus on the Cross? Why would they reject Him who loved unconditionally? Why would they kill Him like a criminal when no crime was to be found against Him?

The Gospel taught me that I did not need to go far, one of those men was in me; my own ignorance and fleshy desire, like a veil, were hiding my face from the truth. I myself was taught in Islam to rely on external things and therefore was unable

---

25 Revelation 19:16
26 Ephesians 6:12.

to see the beauty of Christ's face. I dishonored and crucified Him by putting Him in an Islamic frame and rejected His Gospel. We were never given an opportunity to read Islam's so-called 'rejected Gospel' and see how Christians viewed Christ and why. We disliked if anyone described Him in a non-Islamic way. I had never known that Allah, Muhammad, all Muslim scholars and myself had despised Jesus. All our religious emphasis in Islam was to believe ourselves better than others,[27] to terrorize others,[28] to seize their lands and properties and wives,[29] and to extend the kingdom of Islam on earth. We called all these worldly works spiritual success and more worthy than the works of Christ. We were ignorant and did not know anything about spirituality and truth. We disrespected logic, reason and confidence, and approached non-Muslims with dishonor and hostility. We called our conditional love in Islam better than the unconditional love of Christ.

Alas, I did not know that the supreme desire of Muhammad and Islam had nothing to do with forgiveness, righteousness and spiritual progress and therefore wasted half of my life with the rituals and instructions of Islam. Islam focuses on the world and worldly desires. Jesus gave His life for friends and enemies to draw their attention to love and holiness, but Muhammad did not allow even his own friends express themselves in his presence.[30] He slaughtered his opponents.[31] How could I call Jesus less spiritual than Muhammad? How could Muhammad call himself, but not Jesus, the finisher of God's work?

The prayer of Christ on the Cross revealed all the misinformation and injustices of Islam and also the filth of my heart to me:

---

27 Q3:110.
28 Q5:59.
29 Q33.
30 Q33:36.
31 Q9 (read the whole chapter).

Father, forgive them, for they do not know what they are doing. (Luke 23:34)

No committed Muslim can fathom such forgiveness from Christ. That's why Muslim scholars and fighters have always tried to call Jesus a Jihadist in order to justify their hatred of Jews and others. Time and time again, Yasser Arafat called Jesus the first Palestinian *fedayeen*,[32] trying to relate Him to Islam's sword philosophy against the Jews.

As the veil of hostility had covered my face, it did the same with Arafat's, not allowing him to understand the heart of Christ:

Our struggle is not against flesh and blood, but against…the powers of this dark world and against the spiritual forces of evil in heavenly realms. (Ephesians 6:12)

Christ's war is not with humanity, but with the enemy of humanity, Satan. Satan cherishes ignorance, bigotry, hostility and bloodshed. Christ humbled Himself, left His heavenly glory and appeared among us to save us but not to hate and kill us.

His humble attitudes shamed me for the hostility I had towards Him and His people. I didn't know that the hostility in me was my own enemy too, but He knew. While I was not able to see this enemy in me, Jesus saw its ambush and became a shield for me, against its arrows. Jesus had every right to ignore or reject me, but He didn't. His heart is like a faithful parent's heart that does not condemn his/her child for wrongdoings, but gives a chance and even lays his/her life and wealth in order to protect the child against foes. This is what He did for me:

Surely he took up our infirmities and carried our sorrows, yet we considered him stricken by God, smitten by him, and afflicted. But he was pierced for our transgressions, he was

---

32 David G. Littman, "Yasser's Terrorist Jesus", FrontPage Magazine.com, 11/15/2004.

crushed for our iniquities; the punishment that brought us peace was upon him, and by his wounds we are healed. (Isaiah 53:4-5)

Every sacrifice of Christ turned my heart to my motherland and I cried loud to Him and said, "You deserve to be the Master of my nation. If you open their eyes, they will appreciate what you have done for them."

I remembered a great proverb from my motherland that said, "Never forget even the kindness of an enemy." In my culture (unlike Islamic culture), if a person rescues you from death, you will always feel indebted to him (or her), showing them a special respect. But if you turn your back on him, everyone will complain and say to you, "Is this your response to kindness?" Anytime you see this person, you have an obligation to remind him how he saved your life. You feel proud to call yourself a son, a daughter, a brother or a sister to that person. After I realized what Jesus had done for me, I felt honored to call Him my Savior, Brother, Father, Redeemer, Friend or anything that could express my love and appreciation to Him.

For me, Jesus was no longer a son of jihad who imposes his beliefs on others. He was the Son of kindness, love, holiness, justice, righteousness, wisdom and reason. Through Him, I learnt the heart of God said that real victory in life was not in killing men and women (infidels in Islamic context) but sparing their lives for God. The desire for a person's death is a contribution to the kingdom of Satan, because Satan loves death over life. Now I needed to act against the desires of Satan and lead people to salvation[33] and peace.[34] I found it urgent to align myself with the mission of Christ to save souls, no matter who they were.

---

33 Ephesians 6:17.
34 Ephesians 6:15.

11

My Family Returns

A Changed Man

Back in Iran, my wife was shocked at Iran's worsening situation. Things were worse than she had imagined. Our visa situation had not changed in Turkey but she thought it best to remove our children from such a volatile environment in Iran. My wife and three daughters rejoined me in Turkey in the fall of 1989.

My wife was unaware that I had given my heart to Jesus. I had refrained from divulging my newfound faith for fear that my wife would not come back to me. Life in Istanbul had already been difficult for her. My conversion to Christianity would cause even greater difficulty. In Islam it was dangerous for her to join an apostate husband.

On the day of their arrival, I thanked Jesus for preparing my wife to come back. In response to His kindness, I thought I should talk to her about Christ, but I quickly changed

Daniel's wife and three daughters at Istanbul airport, Fall 1989

my mind when I saw my wife and daughters all wearing *hijab* (Islamic cover). I was afraid my news would terrify and anger my wife and cause her to return to Iran. So, I took them home without saying anything about Christ.

My wife was surprised by my attitude from the first day. I played with our children, showing joy and sometimes sang songs quietly. She thought, "This man never showed joy like this before." She said nothing though, assuming that, within a week, I would resume the typical Islamic life and culture. After the second week, however, she was unable to withhold her curiosity. "What has happened to you," she asked. "Why are you so happy and nice?"

I did not know what to say and looked at her speechless for a few seconds. I was trembling inside and my eyes started to pour tears. I worried what her reaction would be if I told her the reason of my happiness? No doubt that she would be overcome by fear; but would she become angry at me and take the children and go back to Iran? Since I had changed my religion I would not have any authority on my children any more according to Islam. She would be the only authority. She could even destroy my life.

In the midst of these challenges, I cried to the Lord in my heart and said to Him, "Why are you rushing Lord? This is only our second week together! I need more time to pave the ground and reveal You to her slowly and gradually. I am terrified."

While she waited for my response, I said to her, "A great thing has happened to me. I've wanted to tell you before, but I was afraid to upset you."

Our children were quiet, knowing that a conversation between their parents that involved tears was not a good sign.

With amazement she said, "You were afraid to upset me for a good thing? Why? How can it be?"

"Because I was afraid to lose you," I said.

So far, the conversation had not worried her. Telling her that a good thing had happened to me didn't seem to upset her. It just made her curious how a good thing could make her upset.

I asked her to wait for a few minutes. I went to my room and called Jesus for help and then came back with my Bible, which I had kept hidden. I said to her, "Do you remember a few months ago when we were talking on the phone and I told you that I had found a new friend, and you laughed, saying, 'You are very clever at finding friends; The last one you found took your money and ran away. What is this friend going to do to you?"

Still not knowing the name of my new friend, she smiled at the recollection of the conversation. Then I told her, "My new friend is Jesus. I gave my heart to Him, and I have learned from Him to show respect to you and love you."

She was frightened, believing it would not matter that I loved her if we were killed. I was an apostate under the law of Islam and she had also joined an apostate spouse. "Why didn't you tell me this on the phone?" she asked.

"I was afraid you would become angry and wouldn't want to come."

"What about Muhammad (a fellow Iranian citizen from our hometown who was in Istanbul, although not his real name)? Does he know about your conversion?"

"Yes, he knows this," I said.

She began to panic. "What if he broadcasts this in our hometown? Why did you do this to me? What will happen to my family in Iran?"

"Please don't be afraid," I told her. "The message of Christ is not bad news to frighten people. We were misinformed about it. It changes people's lives for good. You see the change in my life. Isn't it nice that your husband no more considers you inferior? You must not be afraid. Let us read the words of

Christ together; you will see how beautiful they are and how they will strengthen you."

Unreceptive, she used an Azeri idiom that expresses unhappiness and the close of a conversation for bad, "The one who goes to hell desires a friend to accompany him."

I worried that she might use my conversion as an excuse to return to Iran with our children. She knew that I was automatically disarmed of guardianship over our children by leaving Islam and becoming a follower of Christ. I would not be the one who dictates at home anymore; she was now the leading parent according to Islam. She could leave me. She could destroy my life and she could do everything in her power to save her and our children lives from the penalty of Islam.

My wife wasn't a committed Muslim however. She had lost her zeal shortly after our marriage and then after my death sentence. She acted like a nominal Muslim. She also became skeptical of other religions, believing there couldn't be much difference. Her father was an atheist, a fact known only to his family and a few intimate friends. As a committed Muslim, she should have followed the instruction of the Quran[1] and reported her father to Islamic authorities, but she did not.

She had been brave enough to accept her father's unbelief and keep it secret. She knew that I did the same despite my zeal for Islam. With this background, it wasn't necessarily my conversion that bothered her, but the penalty of apostasy in Islam. I could be writing our death sentence, or causing us to lose the guardianship of our children, or my wife could possibly leave me and return to Iran.

Additionally, she had not told me of her own trials in Iran. Neither her family, nor mine, or our friends showed her much favor for various reasons. They included the unexpected nature of her return, leaving me for an extended period of

---

1   Q9:23 and 123.

time, and the financial burden of looking after her and our three daughters. She learned of increased corruption in Iran during her stay as well. She didn't want our daughters to grow up in such an environment. The Ayatollah Khomeini had legitimized embarrassing things in marriages, short marriages, and in other non-marital relationships, opening the door to immorality for Iranians. Islam considered them blessings however. No matter what Islam called them, they were immoralities to the Iranian culture. Jesus used these bitter experiences in Iran to bring my wife back to Turkey and keep her there with me.

I didn't know what was going on in her head, whether she would leave me or stay. The fear of her leaving stole my peace. Despite my fear, I relied on the sovereignty of Christ, praying constantly for my wife and daughters.

There is no one to change her but You, dear Lord. I want her and my children to know what You have for them. Please reveal Yourself to them so that they will have a personal encounter with You and understand that they need to follow you, not because of me, but because of Your own love and kindness. I haven't been able to be a good husband to her. That's why she is not able to trust me and what I say. If You show yourself to her, she will have every reason to believe in You. This will bring joy to my life as a husband and as father of our children. Almighty God, Your Word says, "Believe in the Lord Jesus, and you will be saved—you and your household" (Acts 16:31). That's why I am speaking to You with a simple and childlike heart and waiting upon You for the fulfillment of Your promise.

Marital Struggles

Throughout our marriage there was always tension between me and my wife over certain issues. My wife decided to marry me so that, together, we could live and fight for the destruction of infidelity and for the spread of Islam. Shortly after getting married she became interested in living a normal life however. Our second problem was a struggle over leadership at home.

My wife came from a more tolerant and maternalistic family, but I was from a strong authoritarian paternalistic family. She wished me to have her consent in everything, contrary to my desire and the instruction of Islam. Our third marriage problem arose when I became unemployed and poor as a result of my opposition to the mullahs and therefore had no choice but to take her and our eldest daughter to live with my mother in the village where I grew up. The limited lifestyle of the village made her unhappy. Later on, when I was caught by the mullahs, she took our daughter and went to the city to live with her parents. She was alone then and without marital tension able to think about the future of her and our daughter.

Now, after joining me again in Turkey after several months, my situation seemed worse in my wife's eyes. First I lost money to my business partner. Then I lost my religion, becoming an apostate and threat to the family. I was trying to surrender my authoritarian leadership and the legacy of my father and Islam to the Cross. Her passion for leadership escalated. Sadly, this is typical of the Middle-Eastern Islamic authoritarian lifestyle. Somebody must be on the throne of tyrannical authority. If the husband comes down the wife will take over power. Real friendship and partnership has no place in an Islamic family.

The Lord allowed her to practice a bit of authoritarianism so that she could understand the patience of Christ in me. Sometimes it was so difficult for me to bear the pressure; my flesh was trying to take me back to my old life and harm her again. Praise be to Christ, the source of absolute patience, Who convicted and counseled my soul and helped me to keep my faith in Him and grow.

She was able to see the changes in me through my patience and calm attitudes. She became happy to have a calm and caring husband. She even became envious of my peace and patience. But her biggest obstacle was her fear of my evangelism now. I wanted to tell family and friends of my faith in Christ as soon as possible but she was afraid if the news of my conversion spread to Iran, her family would be in danger.

Every day she was more amazed at the changes in my life. Her pride would not allow her to express it though. She was wondering whether Jesus had such a mighty power to change a high tempered man. Secretly she started reading my Bible. One night after I had gone to bed she opened the Bible randomly and read the following passage:

> ... *a man will leave his father and mother and be united to his wife, and the two will become one flesh* (Matthew 19:5).

She loved that. Unlike the Quran, the Bible had made it an obligation for a man to leave his parents' house for marriage. In the Middle-Eastern tradition women must leave their father's house for marriage. After we got married, while I was not in prison yet, we rented a room from her parents and lived with them. She was so happy. When things went bad and we had no choice but to go and live with my mother in the village she was always unhappy. Now my wife was happy to find support in the Bible, "a man must leave". She was also amazed that Jesus did not believe a man could have more than a wife.

One time I awoke in the middle of the night and realized that she was not in bed. I got up to look for her. To my amazement, I found her reading the Gospel.

Back in Iran, while we were practicing Muslims and in power, she was not interested in reading Islamic books. This is the case with many Muslim women. They find in these books that they are lesser than their husbands, they are property, can be beaten, and their husbands can bring many wives into the marriage. Husbands can also have short term marriages whether for a day, a week, or a month. I put pressure on my wife to read Islamic books and learn about my rights and how to deal with other wives if I wanted to marry again. She however didn't show any interest in reading such books. Her resentment was partly due to the influence of Iranian culture. Polygamy had not yet publicly been accepted by Iranians and there was still cultural pressure to have one wife and avoid more marriages.

However, once disinterested in reading my preferred Islamic books, she was now reading my Gospel. She was reading the Gospel of Matthew chapter 19. "Oh, you're reading the Gospel in the middle of night," I said.

"It is not your business," she said, smiling.

"Ah, Matthew 19; every woman loves this chapter."

Still smiling, she said, "Don't bother me. Go back to sleep."

"Yes, your majesty," I said to her.

When I got to the bedroom I jumped up and down like someone who gets a touchdown in a football game and said to Jesus, "Yes, glory be to Your Name! You know how to touch hearts. Oh, thank You so much." I cried for joy, knowing that any Muslim who crosses the first obstacle and starts to read the Gospel would want to read more. This was also the case with my wife.

Personal Proof

Jesus' respect for women, lifting them up to the level of men, touched my wife's heart and paved the way for her to read the Gospel and evaluate its words. In the meantime, I encouraged her to join the Christian women's meetings. At first, she was hesitant to have contact with Christians, fearing retribution from Muslims. She made excuses to avoid meetings or go to church. The women from the congregation gave up asking, not wanting to bother her anymore. At a church picnic the women invited her to their meetings again. Though she was apprehensive, she accepted their invitation, speculating that if she did not like the gathering she would find another excuse not to go again.

As was usual at the meetings, the women first shared their previous week's experiences with the Lord. A few ladies said that the Lord had spoken to them. She was amazed, thinking,

"Who is this Lord who speaks to women? The Lord does not speak to women in Islam."

Intrigued, she wanted to know more about this God who does not look at gender, but at the heart. She was amazed when she discovered that there were prophetesses and female evangelists in the Bible. God used both men and women for the salvation of people.

To her surprise, she enjoyed her first meeting and continued attending. The Christian faith gradually made sense to her; she began to think that if Jesus was the true God, she wanted to experience Him personally. Again and again, she said to Jesus, "If You are the living God, do something to me or show Yourself to me so that I can have personal proof."

Early one morning I awoke and saw that she was already up. "Couldn't you sleep?" I asked.

"I slept well," she said. "But I had a dream about Jesus."

"A dream about Jesus? What was it?" I asked.

She recounted her dream. She was walking with Jesus and several other women in a beautiful green field where the grass was knee high. As the others kept walking, she stood back and noticed a deep valley before her. Afraid of falling, she refused to follow them. Jesus told her, "Do not be afraid. Just take your first step." As she took her first step, the valley was lifted up and made level with the field, and she walked on with Jesus.

Amazed, I rushed to get my Bible. I told her that her dream was written in the Bible:

> *Every valley shall be raised up, every mountain and hill be made low; the rough ground shall become level, the rugged places a plain. And the glory of the Lord will see it. For the mouth of the Lord has spoken.* (Isaiah 40:4-5).

As I read this passage and a few others, she began to cry. I asked, "Why are you crying?"

After a pause, she responded, "I think I need to put all my fears and concerns in the hands of Christ. He is saying that He will level my ways and will heal me of my fears." The dream helped her to hear the call of Christ and open her heart to Him. We were both crying. I called her "Dear" and "Honey" for the first time in our marriage.

Jesus gracefully stepped into our lives and started to pave the way for our spiritual growth. We had to learn a lot to open ourselves to the love, joy, patience, kindness, goodness, faithfulness, gentleness and every other fruit of the Spirit of Christ[2]. We had grown up in a dictatorial environment where family problems are not solved by mutual consent and kindness. After we accepted Christ, though we were convicted to live according to our faith in Him, the pressure of home culture failed us from time to time. We had to remind ourselves that we were in the kingdom of Christ, where unconditional love was the base. We praise Jesus that we not only survived, but that He has allowed us to influence the lives of many.

Threats

Life in Turkey remained difficult for us, and in some ways it became harder than it had been in the past. Before, we had financial and political problems, but now our Christian faith became another problem in an Islamic country. Several harsh experiences taught us to put our full trust in Christ and live under his sovereign power. He saved us from three different threats.

One day, a committed Muslim Turk approached me and said that I did not deserve to continue the guardianship over our children and they would take our children from us very soon. I could not tell my wife this, fearing that she would be terrified as I was. But Jesus spoke to my heart that he was sovereign over all, including our children. He spoke through an amazing

---

2   Galatians 5:22-23.

miracle in one of our daughters. She was four years old at that time. One evening we were invited by an ex-Muslim to his house for a meal. There were some moderate Muslims who were open to the Christian message. We were all sitting on the floor and conversing. A fugitive Iranian pilot was sitting beside me. My daughter was sitting in front of me, leaning on my lap. The pilot asked my daughter, "How are you, beautiful girl?" She answered, "I am well, thank you." She then stood and looked at the face of this man and said to him, "Do you feel emptiness in your heart, sir?" This amazed the man. I was amazed too. Yes, he had great pain in his heart. He was a pilot who had escaped from Iran to Turkey. This was a threat to the Iranian Islamic Government, afraid that this pilot might reveal secrets of the Iranian army to foreigners. The Government was trying to use politics to bring him back to Iran. Eventually, his father and brother were taken to prison. They were told that if he was brought back to Iran they would be released. This issue was a great burden to the pilot. He was afraid that his father and brother would be tortured and harmed because of his escape.

Because of this he was shocked and amazed when my daughter asked him such a question, without knowing his struggles. He asked everyone in the room to pay attention to what our daughter said to him. The people all kept quiet and he asked my daughter, "What did you say to me little girl?" She replied, "I see emptiness in your heart, sir." This caused him to raise his voice and cry, and say to my daughter, "Oh, little girl, my heart aches and it is killing me. What can I do?" She told him, "Give your heart to Jesus and he will release you from pain." The pilot listened to the little girl and opened his heart wide and trusted Christ.

This was not only a message to the pilot, but to me, too. Jesus spoke to my heart and said, "Do not be afraid that committed Muslims may take your children from you. I am the Lord of children too. Through the mouths of children I will silence the enemy.[3]"

I learned another lesson about the sovereignty of Christ when I was cleaning our church after a Sunday service. It was my family's turn to collect the Bibles and hymn books, preparing the church for the following Sunday. As we were finishing I saw that our children were tired and I asked my wife if she would want to take them home earlier. Since there was not much left to do she was happy to walk with the children to our rented apartment fifteen minutes away from the church. I was expecting to finish and catch up to them before they arrived home. However, a frightening thing happened just a few minutes after my wife's departure and I thought I might never see my family again.

Twelve young bearded Muslim boys entered the church, coming towards me. This petrified me. They approached and surrounded me. One of them, apparently their leader, asked me, "Were you a Muslim who became a Christian?" I responded without hesitation, "Yes." As he was looking at my face he shook his head to signify that he would deal with me soon. Then he ordered some of his companions to watch me and some to stay at the door to block my way in case I tried to escape. He took the remaining ones to bring down a huge cross that was screwed on the wall in front of the church.

My heart was beating so fast. I told Jesus, "Lord! I hate this fear. I know that one day I have to die. If that day is today, I am OK with it. But I need your peace." As soon as I finished my plea, my heart was at peace and I was no longer afraid. Afterwards, I asked them, "Would you kindly allow me to finish the job until the cross is brought down? Trust me I would not escape. You can lock the door and windows to make sure that I won't be able to escape."

One of them went to the leader and said something to him quietly and then came back to me and said, "You can finish

---

3   Read Psalm 8:2.

your job." I started to collect the books. While I was doing this, he asked me, "Aren't you afraid?" I stopped, looked at his face and said to him, "At the beginning I was terrified. I said to Jesus that I hated to be afraid even if I was to die, and I needed his peace. His peace came to me immediately after my pleas." I started to work again. He then asked me a second question, "Aren't you angry that we are bringing your cross down?" I answered him, "No. I have given my heart to Christ. I am sad, but not angry. By the way, the cross is not mine, it belongs to Jesus Christ."

With my second response the leader immediately appeared nervous and yelled for the others to leave the church. All rushed outside like a stumbling flock with the leader in front. I didn't know whether it was the name of Jesus that terrified them or something that appeared. For a few minutes I stood there astonished. Then I gradually came to myself and asked, "What happened?" I finished collecting the books. I closed the windows, locked the door and walked home.

On the way home I praised God for taking my wife and children away from the church for those terrifying moments. Once again, Jesus proved to me that he was the sovereign Lord and that I had more time on earth. He was also gracious to the pastors and the members who had fellowship in the church. If I had been killed, the authorities could easily blame the pastors or elders for my death, since minority Christians do not have equal rights in Islamic countries to defend themselves.

On another occasion, Jesus saved our family from what could have been a disaster in our lives. One night, one of our friends invited us to his house for dinner. We had a good time there. Our children felt tired so our friend prepared a bed for them early in the evening. Our talks went late into the night and our friend insisted we sleep at his house rather than waking the children and taking them home. The following day after breakfast we went home. Our neighbor, who was a retired army officer, shared what happened in our absence the night before. Someone rang our doorbell at one o'clock in the morning. The doorbell rang for a long time and woke our neighbor and his wife. He opened his window and saw three men in police uniforms. He asked them where they were from and for whom they were looking. One of them answered that they were from the central police department and had come to talk to me. My neighbor said to them, "I am a retired army officer. What you are doing seems strange to me. I am coming to check your police ID." He shut the window and went to the entrance of the building but he couldn't find anyone there.

This story worried me and my wife a lot. I took my wife and children back to my friend's house and then left to speak to some Turkish Christian friends. They reported this to a civil policeman. He went to the chief officer in the central police department and took me with him. From the central police department they checked with all other police departments and nowhere did they find such an issue ordered. Had these three men come to abduct me disguised as police? Who knows? This discovery caused me to move to a Christian friend's apartment which was safer for us.

The Last Plain Macaroni

Our financial situation got worse and worse. It was the summer of 1990 and I was emotionally distraught. We had our last plain macaroni for dinner. I didn't know what to do and where to get help. I had sent messages to some of my friends and relatives in Iran who were in debt to me but I didn't get any responses. I was embarrassed to let our Christian friends know about our poverty. The issue made me very unsettled. I went to our bedroom absentmindedly and put my suit and tie on. My wife asked, "Where are you going?" "Nowhere", I replied. "You have your suit and tie on," she said. I looked at myself with surprise and said, "Oh, I don't know when I put my clothes on."

Since I was dressed, I said to my wife, "Look, I am just going to walk in the streets nearby." I was just about to open the door and go out when our doorbell rang. For security reasons I did not open the door but ran to our window to see whether it was a stranger or a friend. From the window I saw the familiar faces of an Iranian Muslim family.

When I first met Ali, the husband, he told me that his brother from Iran had sent him money, but he had not received it. Because of this he was behind in his payment to the hotel. The hotel manager held on to his passport and he was not able to take his family out of the hotel without it. He was afraid he would be deported by the Turkish police if he did not carry the passport with him. He wanted me to talk to the hotel manager and persuade him to trust him. So I talked to the manager and showed him my passport and student card. I guaranteed him that if he did not pay the money I would pay it in his place. The hotel manager trusted me and gave the passport back to Ali. This made him very happy. He had six children and his wife was pregnant with their seventh.

It was this family that was ringing our doorbell. As soon as I saw them I opened the door, rushing out to welcome them warmly.

Ali said to me, "I see you have prepared yourself to go out. We are not going to stay long."

I responded to him, "Oh, no. I am not going anywhere. We are so excited that you have come."

After half an hour, Ali asked, "Is there any place that we can talk in private?" I said, "Oh, yes. We can go to our room." We went into the room. He said that he finally received his money from Iran. I expressed my happiness, saying that it was wonderful news that his family would be released from financial pressure.

He said to me, "We have never forgotten your kindness in releasing our passport from the hotel manager that day."

"It was my pleasure", I responded.

He said, "This morning, my wife and I went to the market to buy a gift for you as a token of our appreciation for your kindness. We looked at many things but were not able to decide. Eventually, we decided to give the money to you instead, so you can buy whatever you like. I just wanted to give you this $30 in private."

I said to him, "Ali, thank you so much. This is very kind of you. But I can't take your money. You have six children in this foreign country, and another child is going to come soon. You need to keep this money and look after your family. You never know, the situation could change any moment and you may face financial difficulty again."

He insisted I take the money and said, "It is not always money that solves problems. Money without friends will not work well. I would love to have a continuing relationship with you, and I really want you to accept our gift."

I said to him, "Ok. I am going to accept it. Just hold the money in your hand for a few moments. Let me tell you our story and after that I will take the money from you." I continued, "We only had plain macaroni for our dinner tonight and we do not have any money to buy more food for our family. As parents, we have been in pain and did not know what to do. The only thing we could do was cry out to Jesus, expressing our concern to him. Now, you are here in my house saying that you were not able to buy a gift for us and are giving us money so that we can buy whatever we want. I see this as a miracle from our Savior Jesus. By the way, would you be happy if we buy food for our family with this money?"

Ali felt humbled, gave the money to me and started to cry. We felt very close because of the difficulties both our families had. He was also very grateful for how Jesus provided food money for us by making them indecisive about which gift to buy.

After I received the money from him, he pulled out his wallet and grabbed one hundred dollars and said to me, "This is for the church you are going to. Please, take and give it to the church."

I said, "Can I ask you to come and give the money yourself to the church? Sunday afternoon we will come by your hotel and go together."

"I do not see any problem in coming with you to the church," he responded.

So, the following Sunday we took Ali and his family to church. They continued to go to the church after that day.

Ali's $30 was a lot of money in Turkey. We were able to live on it for more than a week. This miracle was not only going to feed us, but teach us and many Muslims a lesson. In Islamic countries ex-Muslims are accused of being paid by churches or western countries to become Christians. Ali was shocked to hear that we were poor and did not have anything to feed our children. Later, Ali gave his heart to Christ and was able to witness the spiritual wealth of Christ over poverty.

Menial Work

A week later, one of our Turkish Christian friends, who had been persecuted for his faith in Jesus, told me that he had found a sales job for me in a leather shop. I was so excited that I could now provide for my family. He asked me to be ready the next morning when he would pick me up to take me to the shop. "How should I dress?" I asked him. "Have a nice shirt and trousers on and a tie too if you have one," he said to me. So, the following morning he came and took me to that place and introduced me to the manager of the shop.

But my friend had misunderstood the manager. He did not want a salesperson. He wanted someone to box the goods and carry them on his shoulder to the distributors and to load and unload the trucks. For some reason the manager didn't even question my attire. Certainly, with such clothes on, he should have at least questioned whether I was right for such a job. In any case, he didn't ask me but instead led me to the work area and ordered me to fill large bags in the corner with leather goods, sew them up, and set them in the corner. He finished his instructions and left me with an eighteen-year-old man who was experienced in the job and was expected to be my boss in the absence of the manager.

I certainly would not have accepted the position if I had been asked. In the Middle East educated people avoid this kind of work. It would be uncomfortable with an overqualified person working in such a humble position.

Nobody asked me however, and now I was to start the job. I wanted to leave, but I was afraid that my friend, who took me to this shop, would not understand and be offended. He was a humble, simple man and did not worry about his worldly prestige. He once was a medical student, but couldn't stay away from Christian evangelism and left the university. Like the Apostle Paul, he threw himself into hard labor in order to see the Gospel of Christ preached. Though he was persecuted for the sake of his faith, he was always joyful and excited. He did not mind sleeping in the streets for the sake of Christ if the circumstances necessitated it. I did not want him to know that I, as his friend, was reluctant to work in such a job. So I could not leave.

I began to work and followed the manager's instructions, but I was not happy. While sewing, I unknowingly sewed my tie to a bag. I didn't realize it until I finished, seeing my tie sewed onto the bag at the seam. So I took my tie off, removed it from the bag and put it into my pocket. Late in the afternoon I loaded all the bags onto the truck, making my clean shirt dirty. After I finished the job the manager approached me and said that I had to come in early the next morning to unload a truck.

By this time I had finished all my examinations at the university, but still needed to write my PhD thesis. Now, because of the difficulty of my job and my family's needs, I had to put it aside for a while.

At lunch and break times a few people who worked in nearby shops learned that I was an educated man and had no choice but to work there. I was very embarrassed. That night I was sad and unable to sleep well. I really did not want to return to work. Finally I came to the realization that I was accountable to my family, and they would not mind that I worked in a lower position. I told myself that I had to work there until I was able to search for a better job.

Things began to get increasingly difficult at work, which pushed me to find excuses to leave. The eighteen year old worker made life hell for me in the absence of the manager. He knew that I was a fugitive politician and also a Muslim who had become a Christian and thereby was very vulnerable to risks. He, himself was from a Christian background. I believe that he was afraid if he was nicer to me it could cause problems for him with committed Muslims if there were any in the area.

In addition to this, he was not a very friendly person. He was like a dictator to me. It was more unbearable for me because of our age difference. I was fifteen years older than him. Culturally, a young man like him is expected to respect older people. I could have complained to the manager about his behavior but I was not sure what the reaction of the manager would be. My faith in Christ encouraged me to pray, and wait on Him.

Within a few months many people there heard about Christ; four Muslim businessmen who were customers at the shop came to believe in Christ. The people of the area, who had seen my behavior at work, began to respect me. This also made an impact on the young boy. He came to me one day with tears in his eyes and apologized for his behavior. This brought joy to my heart. I sensed the strong presence of Jesus so many times in this difficult workplace and I grew to understand him better day after day. I had to be tested there to learn how to overcome difficulties with the love of Jesus Christ. It was there that I tasted the sweetness of evangelism for Christ.

A Burden Relieved

One day, while still at work, I was carrying a large load up a hill on my back. I was very tired and did not have enough strength to carry it. I called for Jesus to help and take the heavy load off my back. As I was talking to Jesus I felt the load became very light. It surprised me and immediately I turned and saw my friend, a Korean Christian believer. He was walking behind me and realized that it was I carrying the heavy load. He held up my load and praised the Lord for helping us. As soon as I saw him he told me that Jesus would take the heavy loads off our backs. "Amen," I answered with joy and tears in my eyes. The coincidence and conformity of his prayer and mine made me very excited and joyful in the Lord for His provision.

There was a Muslim businessman who had a lot of respect for me. He seemed to always have my back. One day a policeman was disrespectful towards me in the shopping center and he attacked the police, smacking him in the face. This Muslim friend was walking down the road and saw me with my Korean friend. He came forward to greet me and saw my eyes full of tears. He immediately said, "Who has hurt you again? Tell me and I know what to do."

"Oh, no, no. Nobody has hurt me." I told him. "These are tears of joy from Jesus. I was praying to him and he spoke to my heart immediately. That's why I am excited."

With a smile on his face, he said to me, "There you go again about Jesus." As he was leaving, he said to me, "Anything you need, let me know."

While we were walking uphill my Korean friend told me that he had established a tourism company and wanted me to work in his office. He came with me to the shop and with respect said to my manager, "Thank you so much for providing this job for my friend and looking after him. I have come to ask your permission to take him to the new position I have for him in my office. You do not need to pay him for the last few days of this week. I will pay him."

The manager respectfully replied, "We will miss him. But I am happy that you have a good job for him. He deserves more than this. He will get all his money from us." He shook our hands and encouraged me to visit from time to time.

The following day I began to work at my friend's company, while commencing work on my thesis to obtain my PhD.

Without a Country

One of my wife's and my major concerns was our future residential status. At the completion of my studies I would no longer be entitled to a Turkish student visa. One option was that I could get a work visa, if the Turkish law allowed us. However, there were still two other threats that clung to our minds. One was the threats from the agents of the Islamic Government of Iran in Turkey, and the second was the threat of Turkish radical Muslims. So we were unsure of our continued residence in Turkey. We wished to go to a Western country, but it had become almost impossible to obtain a visa due to the difficulties the Iranian Islamic Government had created for other countries. It was not easy for Western governments to distinguish between genuine asylum seekers and the terrorists of the Islamic Republic of Iran.

By then we had built a strong relationship with local Christians and did not feel alone in Turkey. We also had ministry opportunities in our church that helped make us more courageous to withstand difficulties and opposition and teach others to rely on the Lord.

Margaret, an Australian Christian, was in Istanbul to visit an Australian family friend. Her friend's husband was a professor in one of Istanbul's universities not far from our church. The family often visited our church. One Sunday they also took Margaret to the church. After the service I met her and she asked me what I was doing in Istanbul. When I explained that I was doing research in order to complete my PhD she asked if I planned to become a university professor.

"I would love to," I told her. "But I am without a country."

"What about your country? Aren't you Iranian?" she asked.

I explained that I could not return to Iran because of the death sentence on me if I returned.

"That's so sad", she responded. At the end of our conversation, she said, "It has been a pleasure to talk to you." Then she turned and joined some other people. Later, as people were departing, Margaret came to me and asked, "If I sponsor you, would you be interested in coming to Australia?"

I was stunned. "Wow! What a generous offer. Why would you want to do this?" I asked her.

"Well, you need a country, and my country also needs people like you. So, it would be an honor for me to do this."

I told her that we would appreciate it if the Lord led her to grant such a favor to our family. She asked me to provide all of our family's identification papers for her while she was in Istanbul, which I did and included a brief written account of my life. Then I left it in the Lord's hands.

A few months later, I received a phone call from the Australian Embassy in Ankara, Turkey's capital. The voice on the other end of the line explained that the Embassy had received our applications from Margaret and that there were more papers I needed to sign. The applications were sent and I completed and returned them. The Embassy soon called and set a date for an interview.

Our interviewer was the Australian ambassador. After welcoming us, he asked "Do you have money?"

I wasn't expecting that question. I thought *Why would he ask me about money?*

"No sir, we do not have money. Why?"

He responded, "If you do not have money, you will not be able to purchase your family's air tickets to Australia. The Embassy does not have any responsibility for purchasing tickets for those who are granted a visa. Therefore, you need to decide if you want to be interviewed and whether you be able to provide the money."

I told him, "Sir, we are Christians. We believe in miracles. If we get our visas, it means that Jesus wanted us to get our visas. In the same way, if He provides the money to purchase our tickets, it means that He wants us to go to your country. Otherwise, we will do whatever He wants us to do. Would it be possible for you to interview us without the money?" He studied my face for a few seconds and said, "Fair enough. I am prepared to interview you."

For the next two and a half hours, the interviewer asked me and my family many questions. Afterwards he led us to a waiting room and said, "I need half an hour in order to look over your responses again and give you a response."

His request discouraged me because usually a decision wasn't made on the same day. I thought perhaps he might decide to reject our application. When the ambassador returned however, he shook our hands and congratulated us for being granted Australian visas. He allowed us six months to provide the necessary funds. Our surprise turned into excitement and we thanked him over and over. While shaking my hand, he lowered his voice and said, "It was an honor for me to interview you. I am proud that you are going to be a part of my country. My country needs you." His statement humbled and encouraged me.

The Miracle

We received our visas and returned to Istanbul. The following Sunday we shared the good news with our church family and asked them to pray for God's provision. However, by November 1991 we still did not have any funds for our tickets. My wife and I came to a conclusion. "It seems that the Lord does not want us to go to Australia," I said to my wife. "It is twenty days until our visa expires, yet there is no money. I promised the Ambassador that if I was not able to provide the money, I would take the visa back and thank him face to face. But we don't have even money for a bus ticket to Ankara. I'll wait until the last day and call him to ask his permission to send the visa back to him by mail."

As we were talking, the doorbell rang. Through the window I saw several of our Christian friends. When I let them in, one of them placed $5,500 on the table and said, "The Lord has provided your ticket money and He wants your family to go to Australia."

This was a huge surprise. We asked them how they got the money. Where did it come from? I knew that their financial situations were no better than ours. They told us of their sacrifice. For five and a half months some of our church families, including a few children, had been eating only once a day, saving the money from breakfast and lunch for us. They knocked on the door of every Christian they knew and asked for donations.

We were humbled and gratefully accepted their gift. On November 23, 1991, we headed for Australia.

Before our departure from Istanbul some friends advised me to study Christian theology after we settled in Sydney. They knew that I had knowledge about Islam and that my PhD research was about cultures and religions. They encouraged me to deepen my knowledge of Christianity.

12

Australia

Down Under

How grateful we were to Australia for granting us a visa, so we could make a home there. We knew the depth of Australia's help and will never forget its kindness. Our forefathers lived in Iran for nearly three thousand years. A group of Saudi Arabian Muslims invaded our country, strengthened their roots and killed or forced millions of Iranians to leave their motherland in the past fourteen hundred years. We were treated as strangers in our homeland, but Australia opened her arms wide and spent thousands of her tax-payers' money to reserve our dignity and human rights. We were amazed at the caring heart of this nation, leading us to always care for this country and even lay our life for her if necessary. God took us to a country beautiful by nature and people.

Upon our arrival in Sydney International Airport we saw Margaret, our sponsor, with many of her friends, waiting to convey a warm welcome for us on behalf of Jesus and Australia. We were so emotional and honored by such a friendly and caring moment. I was overwhelmed by excitement and unconsciously greeted all men in a Middle-Eastern way, kissing them on their cheeks. They were so gracious in ignoring my mistakes but I knew that we needed to learn and respect their culture.

We were not the only ones to shock them culturally. They shocked us. They wore a very casual dress for this welcoming moment, including the pastor. He wore shorts and had an earring! Our imagination said that a pastor had to dress himself formal or semi-formal. An Iranian pastor was with them and contrary to everyone else at the airport he wore a suit and a tie. He did that to make us more comfortable. Eventually we learnt to wear casual cloths and enjoy Australian hot weather.

Keith and Hilda, an older couple in their 70s, hosted us for two weeks in Berowra, a suburb in the north of Sydney. We stayed there until we could finish the settlement paperwork with the relevant government offices and rent a house. My wife and daughters knew no English, surviving conversations with what little English I knew. Keith sometimes would draw or show pictures to us in order to make his words understandable.

After two weeks Margaret found a rental house closer to her own house and we rented it. Our first day and night in the house were a bit horrifying. While I was washing the dishes in the kitchen in the middle of the day I saw a snake moving on a plant in the front yard. The whole family fell into panic until Keith hurried to our help. He saw the snake and then said, "Oh, it is harmless." "Humless! What is humless?," I asked him. He repeated the word a few times but I was still unable to understand. He asked for a pen and paper. I was able to understand him when he wrote the word on the paper "Harmless". As I saw the letter "r" in the word, I started to say, "Oh, harmless, harmless, emphasizing the letter "r", yeah, I understand it now."

The following night we took our daughters each to their own designated bed in the house. We were happy and excited they could have their own bed and room! My wife and I were also ready for a peaceful night and rest after a long day. We once again praised God for His abundant grace and mercy to our family for sheltering us in Australia.

As we were ready to go to bed we saw a giant spider moving on the window in our room between the glass and fly-screen. This was scarier than our daytime experience with snake since it was night time. I jumped to the window to make sure that there was not a hole any place on the window for the spider to have access into the room. With fear we planned to kill it before it could kill us. The only solution was for me to go out and kill it from behind the fly-screen from outside. My wife said, "What if it sprayed poison on you from a distance. We never know, maybe some of them are on the pathway or on the plants around." I listened to my wife and gave up going out. We looked at each other and didn't know what else we could do. It was around 11pm. After 10pm, you do not call people normally. We had no choice but to call Keith again and wake him up for help. Keith came and saw the spider and repeated the same word, "Harmless," which he had used for the snake. Not only was this scary spider harmless but also good for eating mosquitoes and insects said Keith. The day after he brought a book and showed us many pictures explaining which creatures in Australia were harmless and which ones harmful.

One day, Bill and his wife a couple from Margaret's church, who were in our neighborhood, called me and invited the family for 'tea' at 6 pm. After thanking him, I said that I would call him back after checking with my wife. My wife and I found it strange to be called for tea at 6 pm. This was also our dinner time. With three very young school children we usually ate our dinner earlier so that the kids could go to bed early to be up early in the morning. Since these were our first days in Australia and did not know the culture we did not want to lose this friendship opportunity because of our family set time for dinner. We wanted to have a chance for building a relationship with our neighbors. We decided to have our dinner earlier than 6 pm and go for tea. We did not want to leave our dinner for after because it could become late for our children's bedtime.

My wife made a big meal so that it could hold us longer for a late night. After the meal, we walked to Bill's house. We were welcomed so warmly and thanked for accepting their invitation. Bill's wife had to rush to her kitchen as she was cooking something. We saw that they had set seven plates on the table and Bill was also setting glasses for drinks. My wife and I started to talk to each other quietly, "It seems that they are waiting for some other visitors to come for dinner. I hope they bring the tea for us quicker so that we can leave earlier rather than disturbing their dinner time. Why did they call us for tea if they had called others for dinner?" We did not know what to say, and kept sitting there quietly but nervous for any inconvenience we could cause.

After a short time they put all food on the table and called us to take our seats around the table.

I said, "Oh, thank you so much. We had our dinner and have come for tea only."

With a perplexing face, Bill came closer and said, "But I invited you for dinner."

"I am sorry Bill, you never mentioned anything about dinner. You just asked us to come for tea," I responded.

"Oh, my goodness," Bill said, "I am sorry, we call dinner tea sometimes. If we want to offer hot drink to someone, we say a cup of tea or coffee. I am so sorry; that's my mistake."

Well, we felt so sorry for our precious neighbors to cook a lot of food for us who had eaten till our stomach's almost burst. Our children were so full they were unable to touch the food. Only my wife and I could eat a little bit with them.

Our older daughter was 11 years old, extraverted by nature and able to relate herself to the students in school socially. The two younger ones, 6 and 4 years old, were attached to us parents because of their age, and also the new culture and environment. We experienced their tears in the first days of school and sometimes also shared tears with them. After a few days of struggling with a lack of communication with classmates and also the long hours away from the family, our middle daughter came to us with a solution: "Mum, how about we two stay at home with you and our older sister learn from her school and teach us at home." It was heart-breaking for us that we were not able to grant her days of thoughtful and sensitive planning. We would have loved them to grow in their learning with Australians from the beginning to the end so that they could have a memorable life in the future. They were little and had good opportunities to establish themselves in the Australian culture, appreciate it as their own country and also help us, as their parents, to understand it well.

We were a bit different than our children. We had already established ourselves with the Iranian (and Middle-Eastern) culture. We had a long journey to learn English and the western culture, and find the most appropriate way to be a blessing to Australia.

We missed our families in Iran very much as we had not seen them for years. Different things would remind us of our families and bring back memories in Iran, leaving us emotionally tortured. We sought to reduce our homesickness via building connections with Iranians and in particular with Iranian Christians in Sydney. However, the Iranian culture is a strong family oriented culture and we still missed our families. We prayed to God daily impatiently waiting for the tyranny in Iran to come to an end so that we could go and see our families. We haven't been able to see our families for more than two decades.

My wife's life became so difficult in the first years of our life in Sydney. She heard of the sudden death of her mother, older sister and a couple of her uncles. She was shattered emotionally because she could not be there to see her dear ones in the last moment of their lives. One day, she shocked and terrified us by saying that she was no longer able to bear the pains of separation and wanted to go back to Iran to see her family. "What about if the Islamic Government takes you to prison, tortures you and keeps you as a hostage in order to torture the entire family in Iran and Sydney? Wouldn't it be more torturing to you to be kept away from your children and husband?" I and a few other friends said to her through our tears. She started to weep and say, "Am I not human? I just want to see my family. This is killing me gradually." We praised God who reminded her that if we did not leave our land we would not have freedom; the sacrifice for freedom came to us with the price of leaving our homeland. God gave her comfort and strength so that she could tolerate the pains and rather invest her life in our ministry for bringing the hostile walls of Islamic rule in Iran down, through the love and sacrifice of Christ. She now rejoices over the salvation of millions of Iranians in Iran and abroad.

It will be always difficult for my wife and me since we have our dear ones living in Iran. We always love to see them. We also understand that this world has turned its back on Christ and His followers, and will not be able to give them peace. We knew from the beginning that we would lose everything for the sake of Christ. Sometimes we forget and pour tears, but as the Apostle Paul said, nothing can separate us from the love of Christ[1].

Our first three years were spent learning the language, culture and computer skills in Sydney. As a family, we attended an English-speaking church on Sunday mornings and a Persian fellowship in the afternoon. I began receiving invitations from churches to give a testimony of our journey from Islam to Christ. At first, I would take an interpreter to translate my Persian into English, but gradually my English improved and I was able to speak on my own.

In 1994 I enrolled in a Christian Bible college, and along with several other Iranian Christians, formed an Iranian church in Sydney. While all of us were involved in evangelism, the preaching was done by me and another gentleman who was

---

1   Romans 8:38-39.

also a theology student. As the church grew the pastoral role was given to me. It was not a paid ministry. I accepted the ministry but felt my call from God for evangelism, in which I became fully involved.

At the end of 1996 I graduated from the Bible College and needed to find a job to support my family. I wanted to find a Christian church or organization that would support my evangelistic ministry, but was unsuccessful. So I set out to look for a job that would bring some income for the family. In 1997 I took a part time job at a university as a lecturer of cultural values in an international management course. I taught this course until 2004. I also traveled throughout Australia, and internationally during school holidays. I spoke about our journey, taught Islamic beliefs and created awareness of Islam's plan for the world, in particular the West.

Our Concern for the West

The fraud of multiculturalism and the growth of passive pluralism in the universities and the western societies worried me about our future in Australia. I had a reason to worry. We had escaped the death sentence and were kindly granted a visa to live in Australia, but I saw our future at risk if the game of multiculturalism continued. Committed Muslims had been using it as a channel to enter and establish their Islamic law (Shari'a) in the West. I lived Islam as a radical and a committed Muslim and was aware of the plans committed Muslims had for Australia and all other western communities. They come to the West to penetrate and change western civilization, until it collapses, giving way to Islamic rule. Not only was I aware of this plan but had been a part of it back in Iran. This was not only the plan of Iranian radical Muslims, but the plan of all radical Muslims. The Ayatollah Khomeini was not the inventor of this Islamic plan. He learned this from the Egyptian Muslim Brotherhood, the mother of terrorism in the world.

It was terrifying to my family to see the establishment and growth of their plans in the West. We could not sit idle and watch our new country tolerate the enemies of humanity, without knowing their history and the root of their belief. We had not escaped the hostility of the pious Muslims with the intension of keeping quiet, and allowing their zealous Muslim brothers to establish themselves in democratic Australia while progressively destroying this democracy as they had done in Islamic countries.

It was shocking to us to hear and read that many people in the West believed that Islam carried the same values as other beliefs. They thought Islam was equally worthy of respect and Muslims did not need to assimilate into western culture. More worrying to us was the common belief that no religion or culture in a pluralistic society had to be criticized since all were equal. People were losing their interest in distinguishing the difference between peaceful and terrorizing ideologies since everything was believed to be right and there was nothing to be called the best or absolutely true. You would be called unethical if you challenged Islam. Our children's brains were being filled in the schools and universities that it was a virtue to agree with everything.

Therefore not many people dared to take a stand against anything that Islamists were imposing on the society, simply for the fear of offending someone. Islamists were also taking this silence and indifference as an opportunity to shelter themselves under the umbrella of this altruist notion, and zealously started to fight people like us, who wanted to expose their destructive plans.

It was scary to see that many politicians in the West put their trust in these Islamists and mosque leaders, asking their counsel in regard to their relationship with Muslim communities. This was happening in a time when even many moderate Muslim governments in Islamic countries avoided any consultation with radical Islamists, unless they have no other choice, knowing it is unwise to give opportunity to the radicals. They were not aware that anytime Islamists attain power, they kill anyone who is not with them or opposes them, no matter an ally or else. The Ayatollah Khomeini slaughtered some of his own friends who once helped him and even rescued him from death.

I knew from Islamic sources and by practice, that Islam not only was not compatible with democratic values, it had also instructions for the destruction of these values. According to Islam, Muslims have no right to fit themselves to the values of non-Muslims, but have to force or lead others to change and suit Islamic values. I was a Muslim leader myself and taught how to permeate the infidel western societies, destroy their cultures from inside and pave the ground for the establishment of Islamic law. I understand when we open a door wide to Islam, it will mean the degradation of non-Muslims and their life values. For this reason, Islamists have been able to push and create a divided loyalty in the West and have their own ghettos, courts, swimming pools, etc. Not only this, they have also been pushing non-Muslims to follow their Islamic diets. Some western country governments are pushed to hand over their obituaries to Muslims, so animals are killed in an Islamic way, giving minority Muslims access to halal (prepared in Islamic way) meat everywhere they want. In other words, non-Muslim majorities have to obey the religious traditions of minority (mostly immigrant) Muslims in their own motherlands. Islamists have been trying to stamp their Islamic logo of "Halal" on everything in order to Islamize everything. They ignore the rights of the majority and pronouncing openly that the foods prepared by non-Muslim hands are unclean. Ignoring the rights of majority is contradictory to democracy, but complementary to Sharia.

After the terrorist attack on America on September 11, 2001, demands for my speaking engagements grew rapidly. Eventually, I relinquished my role as the pastor of the Iranian church and became fully immersed in creating an awareness of Islam's agenda. I had never planned to be involved in such a ministry, but after witnessing the progress of Islam in Australia and the West, I could not keep quiet. I felt very obligated to play my role and defend the western democracy against Islamists whose religious institutions and practices were in conflict with the western laws and values.

Unfortunately, committed Muslims had been successful in acquiring western taxpayers' dollars and the endorsement of politicians to establish their discriminating principles in many areas. I was able to anticipate the terrible consequences of their initiatives. I had to do my part and wake up people to their subtle approaches. With their subtlety, these Muslims introduced themselves as peace lovers. They took away opportunities from their western supporters or friends to personally study Islam and see why Islamists couldn't establish peace and a role model democratic society in the entirety of the Middle-East.

I felt a great responsibility to inform these Muslim supporters and friends. I wanted to encourage them to investigate the principles of Islam so they could see Islam's history of brutality in Muslim-ruled lands. It won't be any better in non-Islamic countries.

Committed Muslims are dangerous people to democracy. Deep in their hearts, they believe that they need to use the freedom in the West in order to permeate societies and subject them to Islam. They believe in one path to freedom. People are free to become Muslim; Muslims are free to make others Muslim; but no one is able to leave Islam or oppose Islam. Freedom is appreciated as long as they have opportunity to spread their religion and dominate. They forbid non-Muslims from practicing their religions openly and building their churches or temples in Islamic countries. Under the rule of Islam, no other religions' followers should be allowed to spread their beliefs or build new sanctuaries. Only ancient church buildings have remained in Islamic countries, although some were turned into mosques. Before the rise of Islam in Saudi Arabia, there were even churches in Mecca, now the holiest city of Islam. Non-Muslims, particularly Jews and Christians, are not allowed to step into Mecca anymore because it is pronounced holy and non-Muslims are unclean, according to Islam[2]. Committed Muslims are very well skilled in abusing and undermining freedom in non-Muslim countries. They can build mosques in every corner of non-Islamic countries, but non-Muslims cannot have a similar right in Islamic countries! Muslims build their mosques and Islamic schools everywhere in the West without a challenge. In fact, some politicians have morally or even financially supported the growth of Islam in the West.

In 1994 some Iranians in Sydney complained to the Australian government to stop the building of a mosque financed by the Islamic Republic of Iran. They believed that the mosque would be used as a spy center for the interest of the terrorist government of the Islamic Republic of Iran. Sadly, the Australian government was not able to look deep at this issue and the mosque was built. Soon after its completion, one of its clerics was suspended for deportation to Iran because of subversive activities.

Muslim leaders have been using their oil revenues for the establishment of Islamic tyranny in the West by building mosques, schools, and Islamic centers. Middle-Eastern oil has become like a gradual death sentence for Western countries. They used their power, wealth and tongue in the Zoroastrian Iran, Coptic Egypt, Catholic Syria and Lebanon, and Hindu-Buddhist Indonesia and made them Islamic. Now, they are following the same strategy in the West.

Under the pretense of multiculturalism and pluralism, committed Muslims are able to make root and establish themselves stronger for the destruction of freedom. This includes multiculturalism and pluralism. Pluralism is an obstacle under the rule of Islam, but can be used by the minority pious Muslims as a channel until they gain power. The lack of knowledge in the West has given them opportunity to cleverly use the Islamic deceitful principles for spreading

---

2   Q9:28.

their false messages and attaining their religious goals. They
have been telling people that:

Islam supports knowledge and reason. It is a just, merciful and
peaceful religion. It believes in freedom and never imposes
itself on others. Yes, there is Jihad in Islam but it is only
spiritual and for internal purification. There is also a physical
jihad in Islam which is only defensive, but never invasive.
Those who fight against Jews in the Middle-East are freedom
fighters. Islam is the only religion that can liberate nations. It
is also the only religion that has liberated women since the
rise of humanity. If Islam governs the western countries, it will
be more democratic than the present situation in the West.
And so on...

We discovered that these statements are just a few examples
of their deceits that were widely accepted in the West. Even
millions of moderate Muslims in the Islamic countries know
that Islam does not have peace with non-Muslims, female
Muslims are the second class citizens, Jews are the number one
enemy because they loudly questioned the prophetic claims
of Muhammad. Westerners are still behind in understanding
these facts of Islam.

Time and time again, I raised questions, similar to the
following, in my conversations with Australians, Europeans
and Americans who looked to Islam favorably:

Is there any democratic Islamic country in the world which
has developed an egalitarian system and tolerated human
rights, freedom of speech and religion? If yes, why has every
Islamic country, even the most moderate one among them,
made the proselytizing of Muslims illegal? Why can Muslims
build their mosques and schools in non-Islamic countries, but
non-Muslims are not allowed to have similar rights in Islamic
countries?

If Islam hasn't been able to produce a democratic country in
the world, how can it be a hope for non-Islamic countries?
How can it be called equal to other religions and beliefs? Why

would many westerners give a space to the authoritarianism of Islam inside their smooth and participative Judeo-Christian culture?

If Islamists were not able to respect the freedom of their own people, how do we expect them to respect freedom in foreign lands? If they are hostile towards their own family members and citizens, how could we, as strangers, dare to open our doors wide to their way of life? If they have religious obligation to be hostile to their own nominal Muslim family members and citizens³, will they be nice to us?

Why do Iraqis, Egyptians, Sudanese, Algerians, Syrians, Jordanians, Palestinians speak Arabic while they are not Arabs by race and did not speak Arabic originally? Wasn't this because Muslims not only wanted to Islamize the natives but to spread their Arabism among them too?

Were Iraq, Egypt, Sudan, Algeria, Syria, Jordan, Palestine, Iran, Spain and India any threat to Muslims in ancient Saudi Arabia when they invaded these countries? How could these wars be called defensive while Muhammad and his successors wrote to the leaders of these countries and threatened them that they wouldn't be invaded if they believed in Islam and subdued themselves to the rule of Islam?

Why does the Quran label non-Muslims as unclean, animals or worst of beasts and sanctions death for them unless they become Muslim?⁴ Is this because of its peaceful nature?

Why do committed Muslims reject Jews and Christians ten times a day during their five times daily prayers?⁵ What kind of peace Muslims can have with Jews and Christians with such a hateful daily prayer?

---

3   Q9:23, 123.
4   Q2:65; 5:60; 7:175-177; 8:55; 25:44; 62:5.
5   Q1:7.

Everybody in the West needs to find the responses to the above questions in order to understand how and in what ways Islamists have betrayed them in their relationships.

Sadly, those who are expected to speak and stand for the truth of Judeo-Christian values in the West, against the invasion of Islam, not only lack the conviction to be effective, but are also being systematically silenced due to political correctness, altruism and multiculturalism. Due to all sorts of threats from Islamists, not only do many politicians remain complacent, they have also become an indirect support to terrorist regimes in the Middle-East against Israel, as a result of their dependency on oil. The western politicians once listened to the voices of their consciences and put all their zeal into helping Jews to reestablish their government in their promised land rescuing them from further hatred and massacres as what happened in Germany and some Islamic countries. But now after five decades, their descendant politicians see the solution in welcoming and strengthening Islam at the cost of Israel and the entire West. Governments have been giving more weight to oil than national security in their lands. For this reason, terrorism has not disappeared but instead grown, for terrorists have become more diligent in the pursuit of their agendas for the destruction of the world.

Sadly, many churches and Christians also have chosen to be quiet. They think that their silence will grant them security. They have forgotten their Master, Jesus, who did not keep quiet against false religions and prophets but laid His life for the truth. What a shame that many churches have disconnected themselves from their root, replaced their love of God and the diligence of their faith with the relativistic values of the world and have become irrelevant to the truth.

There is a great responsibility on our shoulders to hold to the truth sincerely in order to protect our families and communities from expansionist and dangerous Muslims who have unlimited appetite for the destruction of our free and democratic values.

Our Concern for the World

As ex-committed Muslims, we are deeply aware how cleverly-committed Muslims can trap complacent people and destroy their life values. We are unable to keep quiet against this conspiracy, even though our perseverance has cost us a great deal and is going to cost us more. If we keep quiet against the plots of Islam and its agenda for domination, non-Islamic countries will be further deceived and eventually turned into what Iran, Saudi Arabia and other Islamic countries are. If we do not reveal the truth of Christ, Islam will continue shadowing over a billion Muslims, including my own families in Iran, and keep them in the dark. We need to help the world community to understand that Islam is a worldwide threat to anything that is good and non-Islamic.

We now know all about the Islam and Muslim culture so we can help them in any aspect of life. We were called from the dominion of Islam into the Kingdom of Christ to be His light to other Muslims.

No Islamic countries are open to the freeing values of Christ and the democratic values of the West. This is a threat to humanity. The solution for such a threat is the knowledge of Christ. Before they take initiatives and impose their authoritarianism on our societies, we need to open their eyes in order to value human dignity, freedom of choice and equal opportunity. It is our duty to find every channel we can to help Muslims widen the scope of their research, understanding, evaluation and decision making. If Muslims find an opportunity to compare Islam with the faith in Christ, they will leave Islam and Islam will be disarmed.

We praise the sovereign God who has opened many doors for us to reach out to nations. He has also given us a platform in television ministry to speak to millions of Muslims and non-Muslims in the world. Millions of Muslims can now hear our teaching via satellite televisions, radios and websites all over the world. We can tell the stories of Jesus to people in a way that they can identify with Him, rejoice in Him and share their joys with family and friends. It has been overwhelmingly joyful for us to see millions of Muslims and non-Muslims understand the doctrine of Islam personally and find Jesus as their Savior through our ministry. Hundreds of Muslims, especially younger ones, have been coming to Christ every month because of our testimony and teaching. Our stories flow into their lives and they can see that our lives are changed and grounded in the truth, the truth which Islam has not been able to give them. A few of them call us with unethical words and swear words to disappoint or weaken us. They know how influential our ministry is and therefore worry that we will change all Muslims. But even these people do not turn away without our impact. Some of them also came to the Lord Jesus.

Isn't this amazing, that a radical Muslim family could be changed by Christ and used now for the glory of His holy, just, loving and peace-making Name? Oh, it is truly amazing! He has given us His Word to change the world. It is His Word in us to give to the world. It will never fall down but will bring fruits.

Up to this point, the joy of many Muslims finding salvation in Christ has become our power to overcome harassments and attacks with which we are confronted daily. I have been harassed, attacked and threatened by Muslim extremists both verbally and physically in some non-Islamic countries. Terrible things were written in newspapers and websites or told on radios and televisions against me. But, the peace of Jesus Christ has kept me from fear of threats and has encouraged me to become more zealous for His truth.

I praise the Name of my Savior, Jesus, who has brought me to believe that even my martyrdom in Christ will lead thousands of Muslims to accept His truth. Many Muslims will then go to read my blog and my books and give their hearts to Jesus. I love to live for Christ and with His just and loving values. I do not want to die but rather live for the truth. To love the truth and to live for it sometimes necessitates sacrifices, be it our lives, jobs or wealth. We also need to sacrifice so that our children, grandchildren and the future generations can live in peace.

There are some who are self-centered or others who are chained in lawlessness and evil, and therefore hate the truthful and loving message of Christ. We do not wish them to have power over us and our nations. They hate us because we object to their ideologies. Sometimes they find opportunities to impose, threaten, harm or even kill us. But history has proven that Christ will never miss a seed His followers sow; He will grow it. He has used every drop of His martyrs for the salvation of their nations. In the last thirty years the Islamic Republic of Iran has slaughtered a number of Christians. Iran however has never seen the number of Muslims who have come to Christ in the history of Islam in Iran, as seen in the last thirty years. If we eagerly stand for the truth of Christ, He is faithful in bringing the walls of hostility down and establishing His Kingdom through our care, love and sacrifices. He has saved us for this reason.

Daniel and Mary are now reaching out to millions for Christ

Speaking out and revealing the values of Islam are the most influential ways in drawing peoples' attention and encouraging them to hold to the loving and caring values of Christ. Islam and Islamists can be overcome only in the Name of Christ.

I love to express my heart loudly as an ex-radical Muslim, and say that the Truth of Christ is always victorious, has already overcome the evil of the world, taken justice to victory and is triumphant eternally. For these reasons, we press on to make His Truth known and loved by many, including Muslims.

CPSIA information can be obtained at www.ICGtesting.com
Printed in the USA
LVOW04s2320150915

454283LV00019B/234/P